# Hidden Treasures

A Pastor's Journey Navigating Stage IV Cancer

Dan McClure

*I can't imagine what it would feel like if one of my kids were diagnosed with cancer. With that said, I dedicate this book to my mom and dad because one of their kids has been diagnosed with cancer. I love you both dearly and thank you for the unending love, courage, and support you have given to me and my family.*

# CONTENTS

# Foreword by
# Avery Stafford, D.Min.

This is personal for me.

I have known you, Dan, in several roles. When we first met, you were the CEO of a wellness nonprofit corporation in Silicon Valley. You were also a prospective new member of our fifty-year-old church moving into a new neighborhood in a newly renovated commercial facility. I have known you as a city networker, a husband, and dad, a college professor, a pastoral intern, an influential church leader, a skeptic, a Silicon Valley lifer, a prophet, a culture interpreter, a preacher, a Bapticharismatic, a pastor, a cancer patient, and a friend. None of these roles fully capture the essence of the gift you are in my life, quite like a brother.

So, my brother, I want to thank you for allowing me to experience yet another one of your many roles—a writer.

*Hidden Treasures* is your compelling continuing story. It is unapologetically a testimony of God's goodness in your life. While reading it, I thought about Jesus, the master teacher. He drew multitudes of people from all over the Galilean region. He attracted every kind of person from every walk of life. They wanted to know him, and they wanted to hear everything he had to say. It occurred to me while reading your book that I was leaning into your story. I listened to everything you had to say. My engagement in your book was a gift—a moment in time that helped you fulfill your prophetic calling. The gems found on every page will bless readers. Those precious stones will refocus their eyes on God's abundantly nutritious provisions that exist all around us. Every chapter is an invitation to readers to consider Jesus, the pearl of great price hidden in a field yet readily found.

But don't get it twisted. I assure you, my dear brother, Dan, that you are a hidden treasure in our lives. Your pastoral gift is evident in every story, every testimony, every passage of Scripture, and every word of encouragement. You have accomplished more than publishing a book. You have added your voice to the choir of vocalists who want people to live well.

Thank you for *Hidden Treasures*.

Thank you, Pastor Dan, for living well.

"God grant my request. Completely heal Dan from this disease from the top of his head to the soles of his feet. The sooner, the better! In Jesus' name, AMEN!"

**Your brother,**
**Avery**

Avery Stafford, D.Min. is a pastor, professor, recording artist, and author. Look for his latest book release *When Collaboration Mirrors the Trinity: Leveraging Unity to Bless Our World* published by Wipf & Stock.

INTRODUCTION

# Back in Black

I double checked my equipment, making sure I had everything I needed. This was not a time that I wanted to be caught with my pants down.

Room-temperature organic coffee? Check.

Hose clamp? Check.

Bucket? Check.

Enema tube attached to the bucket? Check.

Coconut oil for lube? Check.

AC/DC's "Back in Black"? Check.

I poured the room-temperature coffee into the bucket and made sure the hose clamp was closed. The last thing I wanted was for the coffee to shoot out of the hose before I was able to shove said hose five inches up my backside.

I lubed up the nozzle with coconut oil. I don't like the taste of coconut, so I was glad it was going into my butt rather than into my mouth.

And now, the most important step: "Hey, Google, play AC/DC's 'Back in Black.'"

This may not sound like a traditional treatment protocol for terminal stage IV cancer, but when your doctors tell you there's no clear path forward, you start exploring other options. And as uncomfortable as a coffee enema may be, it's nothing compared to the radiation and chemotherapy I had opted out of.

I opened the hose clamp. Time to party.

## *Song Choice Is Everything*

You may be asking yourself, "Why is a pastor listening to AC/DC? Shouldn't he be listening to hymns and worship music?"

If you have never experienced the joys of giving yourself a coffee enema in the comfort of your own home, allow me to assure you that worship music is not an appropriate soundtrack for this activity.

Don't believe me? Go ahead and give it a try. Shove a tube up your rear, release the hose clamp connected to a bucket filled with cooled organic coffee, and then attempt to hold the flowing liquid in your rectum to the soothing strains of Chris Tomlin's version of "Amazing Grace (My Chains Are Gone)."[1]

This does not work. You can take my word for it.

But if you follow those same steps while blasting AC/DC's "Back in Black,"[2] "Thunderstruck,"[3] and "T.N.T."[4] on your Google Home speaker, you will be amazed by your sphincter's ability to hold in twenty ounces of a caffeinated beverage.

I learned the AC/DC trick the hard way. My first three attempts at a worship-music-inspired coffee enema exploded in a sprinkler shower of poo. You know those sprinkler attachments you can hook up for your kids to run through on the front lawn during hot summer days? The water whips around unpredictably, providing great entertainment for your little ones and easing the misery of a scorching hot summer. Trust me, you don't want similar sprinkler action shooting out your backside.

I was able to hold the coffee in my rectum for about thirty seconds with "How Great Thou Art"[5] playing in the background before I morphed into a mocha crappuccino sprinkler. Floor, walls, ceiling—everything was covered in a caca-coffee combo.

It became obvious I needed music that was a little more bad ass, if you will. And "Back in Black" turned out to be the perfect song to play while flexing my rectum.

The first time I played AC/DC during a coffee enema session, I made it through three songs—"Back in Black," "T.N.T.," and "Thunderstruck." The pumping rhythms and lyrical passion of AC/DC helped me to hold the coffee inside my body while these greatest hits played over my Google Home system.

Three songs. Twelve minutes of music. It wasn't so much a new record as it was a miracle.

You see, God is great, and in this particular situation, "How Great Thou Art" simply cannot compare with AC/DC. God and I have a fantastic and often comical dad/kid relationship. He has never judged me for my song selection in dealing with this sucky disease. In fact, God pointed out to me that when I look to Him, I will in fact find Him every time.

The Holy Spirit revealed to me very early in my diagnosis that cancer was not going to win, and even if it did, Jesus already promised me that I will never die. Jesus took care of death for me already, and I know I have eternal life through Him.

## *Rejecting the Traditional Cancer Playbook*

The Word of God tells us that the enemy tries to steal, kill, and destroy (John 10:10). God, however, is in the victory business, and He taught me along the way how to outrun the devil.

This book is all about victory. I am going to take you on a journey and share with you the hidden treasures God revealed to me about cancer and a variety of other chronic diseases. It is my hope that you will then be able to apply these lessons to your own journey.

The majority of people who are diagnosed and treated by modern medicine tend to adopt the traditional cancer playbook, which they believe will give them the best shot at beating the cancer beast.

In some very welcome cases, patients earn the distinction of being "in remission." According to the American Cancer Society, the five-year survival rate for small cell lung cancer, all stages combined, is 6 percent. For bladder cancer, the five-year survival rate for all stages combined in 77 percent.[6]

We can thank the billions of dollars spent on cancer research and the trillions of dollars in revenue the cancer industry generates for the majority of patients who do survive more than a few years after diagnosis.

However, we also need to consider the fact that one in five people in the U.S. will die from cancer.[7] This sobering statistic remains true despite early detection and diagnostic technology and new drugs and treatments. Even more sobering is the reality that many people die from these drugs and treatments rather than from the cancer itself.

Cancer is a big business. If we found ways to prevent and reverse cancer, we would build a huge dam in the revenue stream of hospitals that admit cancer patients, health care professionals who specialize in the disease, and pharmaceutical companies whose business relies on the side effects of the drugs they manufacture, which then require additional drugs to treat.

Please understand that I am not saying these things in judgment of the people and the companies trying to make a difference. There are fantastic doctors, great companies, and amazing treatments out there, all of which are working hard to save lives.

But you deserve the whole truth—the raw, honest, scientifically-based facts that there are more options available for annihilating cancer than your local oncology department would like to admit.

My wonderful wife, Annette, and I decided we weren't going to push our luck. We wanted to "make our play" through faith in our Creator and through the knowledge we had gained through years of studying exercise and nutrition and working in the health and wellness industry. We wondered if healing from cancer could include finding peace in the chaos.

## More Than a "Shot in the Dark"[8]

We praise God because we discovered very early in my journey that God created a path to preventing and managing cancer. With my terminal diagnosis and no concrete, recommended treatment plan, Annette and I were blessed with the opportunity to take Western medical advice lightly while prayerfully exploring other available options for treatment.

> *My son, if you receive my words and treasure up my commandments with you, making your ear attentive to wisdom and inclining your heart to understanding; yes, if you call out for insight and raise your voice for understanding, if you seek it like silver and search for it as for hidden treasures, then you will understand the fear of the LORD and find the knowledge of God.*
> *—Proverbs 2:1–5 (ESV)*

I want you to know that there is no exact science for tackling chronic disease. There is however an opportunity for all of us to learn the deeper truths that this journey forces us to dig up. After each chapter, homework assignments will give you a starting place for doing your own digging as your journey through life with a chronic disease. It's time to start digging up the *hidden treasures* on your path.

CHAPTER ONE

# Hidden Treasure #1: Divine Appointments

I have to tell you that your cancer is terminal. If you treat it, you will have approximately two years to live. If you do not treat it, you will have three to six months.
**—My oncologist**

*Have I not commanded you? Be strong and courageous. Do not be afraid; do not be discouraged, for the LORD your God will be with you wherever you go.*
*—My God (Joshua 1:9)*

The date was October 30, 2017. I was overflowing with joy because my daughter was hitting a milestone double-digit birthday. Sierra was turning 10, and we intended to go all-out to celebrate her.

I was setting up for her party in the park about a mile from our home. We had food and drink tables, her favorite chocolate cake with white frosting, and—the main event—bubble soccer.

Bubble soccer is a hoot. Each player hops into their own gigantic, transparent, inflatable ball and straps it on so that just their legs stick out the bottom. You then drop a soccer ball on the ground and stand back as fifteen pre-teen girls bounce into and off of each other as they try to kick the soccer ball into the goal.

Each top-speed collision provided valuable lessons in potential versus kinetic energy as the girls crashed into each other and then went flying backwards. I couldn't help thinking of the scene in *Willy Wonka and the Chocolate Factory* where the Oompa-Loompas diligently roll away Violet Beauregarde after she swells into an enormous blueberry.[9]

I was smiling and watching the kids play, contentedly singing one of the Oompa-Loompa songs to myself, when my phone rang.

I should've let it go to voicemail.

## *Not the News I Was Hoping For*

I glanced down at my phone mid-song to see who was calling me and recognized my doctor's number. Six months earlier, I had visited my general practitioner so she could check out some inflammation that I was sure was a slight hernia just above and to the right of my joystick. Why be anatomically correct about things when euphemisms are more fun?

After examining the inflammation, my doctor suggested I have a CT scan. The results of the scan showed that there was no hernia, but it did reveal some dark spots along my spine and hip bones. My doctor assured me that it was most likely arthritis, but she recommended that we do another CT scan in six months. No big deal, right?

So, I answered the phone. And I was not expecting to hear what my doctor told me:

"Hi, Dan. It looks like it is potentially bad news. The dark spots on your spine and hip have grown in size. It seems that it is most likely cancer. I ran these results by the oncology department and asked them if it is treatable, and they assured me that it is. We'd like you to come in for a PET scan and some additional testing. Do you have family and friends who can support you?"

If you have been told by your doctor that you have cancer, I know you have empathy for this moment. It's hard to fully express the rush of emotions I was experiencing in my mind and my body as these words traveled from my cellphone to my ear and established contact with my brain.

I wouldn't wish this news on anyone. I felt so light-headed, I thought I was going to faint right there on the sidelines. I had to compose myself and walk some distance away from the laughing girls crashing into each other on the soccer field.

Annette was busy keeping the other parents engaged in conversation while their daughters played. I vaguely remember telling my wife about the phone call I had just received, but I don't remember her reaction. After I hung up with my doctor, everything was a blur. I just remember trying not to pass out.

## *A Divine Interruption*

But I do remember something else that was very unusual. As soon as I told my wife the news, I looked across the soccer field and saw Claudia, a homeless woman I had chatted with earlier in the day.

Claudia had been struggling with drug addiction, and this park was a bit of a hotspot for drug deals. I had just prayed for her that morning: "Come, God, and break this brutal drug addiction plaguing Claudia."

As soon as I saw her across the field, something snapped me out of my own post-phone-call pity party of anxiety and fear. My thoughts quickly moved from the cancer threat to compassion for this sweet friend. My problems—even this new and terrifying issue—immediately became secondary to her addiction.

I walked over to Claudia, and she seemed surprised to see me again. I pointed out my daughter and her friends, and Claudia gave her wishes for a happy birthday.

I felt that it was no coincidence we saw each other twice in the same day. God cares about her deeply, and He wants to set her free from her addiction. I decided to let her know that my life had suddenly taken a challenging turn and that God wants me to know that He cares about me, too. Claudia stepped into my life at this exact moment, and I was wonderfully distracted from my own worries and challenges.

I shared all of this with her, and we hugged each other and prayed for each other. It was a holy moment and a divine appointment. This wasn't a coincidence. It was providence.

You see, God promises us that He will be with us wherever we go. We just need to be aware of His presence and have confidence in Him whether we sense Him or not.

## *What Flavor Is My Cancer?*

Over the next ten days, I became a lab rat. I peed in cups, had blood siphoned out of my veins, accepted radioactive injections, had fingers shoved up my butt, and my testicles poked and prodded by men and women I had just met. I had a piece of my hip removed, bent over for sphincter needles, had a brain MRI, and allowed every single blemish on my body to be analyzed.

Worst of all, I had a camera shoved into my joystick so the doctors could take a closer look at my bladder. I still have PTSD from that last experience.

After all these tests, not a single doctor could locate the primary source of my cancer. This was significant because the primary source determines what specific evidence-based protocols the oncologists would follow. If I had brain cancer, they'd use one treatment method, while if I had bone cancer, they'd use another. Lung cancer, breast cancer, prostate cancer, blood cancer—there's a protocol for every flavor.

My problem was that even though my cancer had spread, they couldn't find where it all started. All they could say was that my cancer was stage IV and that it was terminal based on the growth of the cancer from one CT scan to the next.

So here was my official diagnosis: non-primary stage IV terminal cancer. "Thank you for your business."

## *Exploring Our Options*

Meeting a new specialist every other day and having all these tests could've scared the snot out of my wife and me, but an interesting thing began to happen.

We started celebrating every time a doctor told us they couldn't find the primary cancer source. We began to hand our fear and anxiety over to God and trust that He was doing something different and unique in our situation.

Jesus said in John 14:27, "Peace I leave with you; my peace I give you. I do not give to you as the world gives. Do not let your hearts be troubled and do not be afraid."

By the time we met with an oncologist in early November 2017, we were not afraid. We knew God had a plan. We just weren't sure how He was going to use us to execute His plan. But what we could do was take ownership over this journey and refuse to let the world drive the direction of the diagnosis.

Our first oncologist was all gloom and doom—so we fired her. Yes, you can do that with doctors. You don't have to stay with a medical professional who isn't supportive of you and doesn't have your best interests at heart. This was the same doctor who gave me three months to two years to live. Bye bye!

Annette and I did some research online, and we discovered an oncology team at Kaiser Permanente with stellar patient reviews. The doctor we liked the most happened to be the head of the department—and was also completely booked. So, we decided not to be in a hurry and to wait for an open appointment.

That is the exact opposite of how oncology tends to operate. Once you have been diagnosed, most oncology departments rush you to schedule chemotherapy, radiation, and/or surgery as soon as possible.

The truth is that the cancer didn't just show up overnight, so you do have some time to ponder and research before making any rash decisions. That is exactly what my wife and I did—especially my wife. Annette quickly became a subject-matter expert in all things cancer. She also became my sounding board and my advocate for discovering the truth about this disease.

Not only did we research how to treat cancer, but we also researched the disease itself and began to understand how stress, environment, and diet can contribute to its development.

Here's one more crazy thing about all this: I had been teaching cancer prevention and prevention of other chronic diseases for more than twenty years. I had focused on the importance of a plant-based diet, regular physical activity, stress management, and methods for creating and maintaining healthy environments.

As a result, everything that Annette and I were discovering about reversing cancer had already been deeply rooted in us for many years. I just wasn't walking my talk.

## *Walk This Way*

God called me to pastoral ministry at the age of 43, which required transitioning from being a wellness professional to leading a church. This transition gave me an opportunity to sit on my backside, to eat more meat, fat, and sugar, and to stress over the challenges of running a ministry.

By the time of my diagnosis, I weighed 210 pounds. At six feet and three inches, many people would say that I was not overweight, but I know I was pushing my health limits.

Looking back at photos from that time, I'm shocked at how sick I look. I had a red face, a growing belly, and sore joints. I was not at peace. I was easily angered, and I wasn't sleeping well. I created an environment in my body that allowed cancer to feed and grow, grow and feed.

I do not take it lightly that I have been trained to help guide people and communities to a place of optimal health. I have a master's in kinesiology, which is the study of human movement, with an emphasis in gerontology, the study of aging. Annette and I both have degrees in exercise physiology and nutrition.

The Lord was now giving my wife and me an opportunity to apply to our own lives what we had been teaching. He was combining our mind, body, and spirit knowledge in order to increase our faith in His creation.

God has given every person on the face of the earth the tools and resources to live an abundant life of health and wellbeing. There is no reason to be afraid of cancer. More often than not, cancer is a symptom of the poor mind, body, and soul choices we have been making.

Whether you have been diagnosed with a chronic disease or you simply want to live in abundant health, you will benefit from learning the necessary steps for balancing out your life, which will be our focus in the upcoming chapters.

# Chapter One Homework

**Question:** Describe your experience and the events surrounding when you or a loved one was first diagnosed with your chronic disease. What was that like for you? What did you think and feel? How did you respond to, and what steps did you take after, the diagnosis? Did you take time to process and research? What would you do differently if you could? How does your current thinking impact the choices you can make for yourself in this process today and moving forward?

_____

_____

_____

_____

_____

_____

_____

_____

_____

_____

_____

_____

**Question:** There is evidence of God's involvement in your life all around you. Look back over all you have experienced since you or your loved one was diagnosed. Where do you see God at work?

_____

_____

_____

_____

_____

_____

_____

_____

_____

_____

_____

**Action:** Hand your fear and anxiety over to God and trust that He was doing something different and unique in your situation. As an exercise of faith, every time doubt, fear, and anxiety start to rise—or every time there seem to be no answers to your situation—choose to celebrate. Praise God even, and especially, when you don't understand.

## *Chapter One Notes*

_____

_____

_____

_____

_____

_____

_____

_____

_____

_____

_____

_____

_____

_____

_____

_____

_____

_____

_____

_____

_____

_____

CHAPTER TWO

# Hidden Treasure #2:
# God Is a Nutrition Expert

*And God said, "Behold, I have given you every plant yield-*
*ing seed that is on the face of all the earth, and every tree*
*with seed in its fruit. You shall have them for food."*
**—Genesis 1:29** *(ESV)*

*Then the angel showed me the river of the water of life, as*
*clear as crystal, flowing from the throne of God and of the*
*Lamb down the middle of the great street of the city. On*
*each side of the river stood the tree of life, bearing twelve*
*crops of fruit, yielding its fruit every month. And the leaves*
*of the tree are for the healing of the nations.*
**—Revelation 22:1–2**

The doctor of the future will give no medicine but will
instruct his patient in the care of the human frame in diet
and in the cause and prevention of diseases.[10]
**—Thomas Edison (1847–1931)**

Have it your way![11]**—Burger King**

My favorite baseball team is the San Francisco Giants.
The last time my family and I visited the ballpark, they

were playing the Dodgers. My son, Cayden, and I can't stand the Dodgers and it takes extreme self-control during the game not to join the crowd with the rivalry chant, *"Dodgers suck! Dodgers suck!"* After all, I am attempting not to encourage Cayden to express feelings with four letter words—but the Dodgers really do suck.

As I looked around the sold-out stadium of nearly fifty thousand people, I thought to myself, "This many people will be dead by the end of the month."

No, I'm not some creepy terrorist with dark intentions. I was just doing calculations in my head. Can you imagine if there were a terrorist attack on a baseball stadium and fifty thousand people lost their lives? This country would never be the same. The entire world would mourn this catastrophic loss of life.

Well, every month, cancer launches a major terrorist attack on the United States. According to the National Cancer Institute—based on the reported cancer incidence and mortality from 2017 and 2018—there are approximately 608,570 Americans expected to die of cancer in 2021. That is more than 50,700 people expected to die each month from cancer in 2021. That amounts to approximately 1,660 people per day.[12]

More Americans died of cancer in 2018[13] than in World War I,[14] World War II,[15] the Vietnam War,[16] and the September 11th[17] attacks combined.

Is it just me, or does it seem like we're losing a daily war to cancer? We spend billions of dollars on treatments, but no one is considering the root cause, let alone a real solution.

Our battle tactics are not working. Drug therapies, state-of-the-art hospitals, fancy equipment, medical research, teams of specialists—all failing to gain true ground.

What if cancer were preventable and treatable? What if you found out that thousands of people are healing from cancer by taking a holistic approach that combines global philosophies and medical models?

What if you discovered a true medical model where the only side effects were abundant joy, peace, perseverance, character, grace, love, and hope?

Keep reading!

### *God Made Dirt—and Dirt Don't Hurt*

One great way to prevent cancer is to eat foods that grow from the dirt. I can't seem to find the verse in the Bible that says, "God created Oreo cookies, donuts, pepperoni pizza, and triple bacon cheeseburgers, and they will be yours for food."

The junk we stuff down our pie-hole is contributing to our immune system's inability to fight cancer. Are you ready for a shock? Every one of us has cancerous cells in our blood stream. And cancerous cells love sugar, starches, and animal protein.[18]

If your body is constituted of poor food choices, you are at risk of inflammation in your body. Researchers have determined the link between inflammation and cancer. If we make healthy food choices, like increasing vegetables and fruits, we help our bodies reduce inflammation.[19] With greater levels of inflammation, cancer may purchase real estate on your bones, brain, breasts, or balls—a real bummer if it blossoms bigger and bigger. Add daily stress and worries as a digestive dessert, and cancer will start buying up new properties on multiple organs.

I just described majority of the U.S. population.

Now that you understand the physiology, what's next? First off, stop eating bacon-wrapped Oreo pizzas. That's what I was doing, so I stopped.

Below is a list of foods that I could scarcely stand to hear mentioned, as I missed them dearly when I switched to a whole food plant-based lifestyle in December 2017:

- French dip sandwiches
- Spicy chicken wings
- Hawaiian pizza
- Corned beef (especially in March)
- Hot open-faced turkey sandwiches with gravy
- A &%@#ing steak
- Mint chocolate chip ice cream
- Egg sandwich on a toasted bagel with bacon and pepper jack cheese

Even typing this list makes me angry. First, the standard American diet—featuring foods that may contribute to chronic inflammation—was my staple. Second, in all my wellness training and education, I was never taught about the massive impact of increasing one's intake of plant-based foods for preventing and managing chronic disease.[20]

Sure, I understood that too much red meat is bad for your heart and that fat and cholesterol from animal products are not good for you. But I was not diagnosed with coronary artery disease. I was diagnosed with metastatic cancer that spread to my bones.

Because I was exercising on a regular basis and my cholesterol levels and blood pressure fell within normal ranges, I never imagined that my massive consumption of animal protein was impacting my health. Well screw you, world, for hiding this science from me for so many years.

## *From SAD to Healthy*

You should eat foods that grow from the ground and drink liquid that falls from the sky. If everyone on the planet followed these two dietary guidelines, we wouldn't be spending trillions of dollars each year to manage the symptoms of heart disease, cancer, and diabetes. [21]

In the creation story found in the very first chapter of the Bible, God told mankind, "I give you every seed-bearing plant on the face of the whole earth and every tree that has fruit with seed in it. They will be yours for food" (Genesis 1:29).

The science community supports what God said with evidence-based nutritional research. In fact, according to a study published in the Journal of the American Medical Association, the number one cause of death in the United States is the Standard American Diet (SAD).[22]

If you don't know what foods make up SAD, I would suggest that you track your food intake for a week. Odds are, your diet consists of hamburgers, pizza, tacos, donuts, soda, processed meats, excessive alcohol, French fries, chips, and anything else you can heat up in a microwave or buy from a drive-through. God didn't mention any of these food items in Genesis 1.

Americans are falling drastically short of the daily recommended two servings of fruit and three servings of vegetables. According to the CDC, only 12.2 percent of U.S. adults eat the recommended amounts of fruits, and only 9.3 percent eat the recommended amounts of vegetables. Among the adolescent population, only 9 percent meet the fruit recommendation, and only 2 percent meet this minimum recommendation for vegetable consumption.[23]

Unfortunately, to prevent disease, the recommendation for fruit and vegetable consumption should be doubled to ten or more daily servings.[24] I don't know the exact numbers, but I would guess that less than 2 percent of the U.S. population would meet this recommendation.

Now that my family and I have switched to a whole food plant-based diet (WFPD), we are easily meeting this produce recommendation. Please know that a WFPD is just one of the steps I took to slow the cancer. There are additional strategies that I will cover in the following chapters.

Before I do that, however, I'd like to give you a snapshot of a typical day of eating if you want to transition from SAD to WFPD.

**Breakfast**

- 16 oz. smoothie or fresh juice
- ½ cup of oatmeal with ½ cup of blueberries, 1 tsp of cinnamon, and ¼ cup of seeds (flax, chia, pumpkin, sunflower)
- 1 whole fruit (apple, orange, or pear)
- Organic coffee

**Lunch**

- Large green salad (greens, onions, tomatoes, mushrooms, walnuts, pine nuts, cucumbers, beets, organic vinaigrette dressing)

*or*

- Vegetable burrito (spinach wrap, cooked vegetables, black beans, brown rice, salsa, avocado)
- Alkaline water (I drink this throughout the day)

**Dinner**

- Plant-based soup or any plant-based Instant Pot recipe
- Tomato, avocado, and organic pickle sandwich on toasted Ezekiel bread with organic mustard

Switching to a WFPD has not only helped to slow my cancer. It's helped me to feel better overall. I have more energy, more restful sleep, and an improved quality of life in general.

Our lives change for the better when we start doing things God's way and living how He intended us to live. And reimagining our diet is only the beginning. There are so many more benefits to come.

If you are looking for a reliable source of healthy information for fighting cancer, one of my favorite resources and a plan I followed early in my diagnosis can be found on this website: www.chrisbeatcancer.com.

# Chapter Two Homework

**Question:** Does your lifestyle support healing? Do your food habits support your body's optimal function to help the healing process?

_____

_____

_____

_____

_____

_____

_____

_____

_____

_____

_____

**Question:** Do you eat the daily recommended two servings of fruit and three servings of vegetables? What about the recommendation of ten or more daily servings for disease prevention? What changes can you make to start working toward meeting this recommendation?

_____

_____

_____

_____

_____

_____

_____

_____

_____

_____

_____

**Action:** In a notebook or journal, track every aspect of your food intake for a week. What patterns do you notice? What do your food habits reveal to you? After you track it for a week, follow up by making a new daily meal plan similar to my whole food plant-based diet (WFPD) example. Feel free to tailor your plan to your specific nutritional needs.

# *Chapter Two Notes*

_____

_____

_____

_____

_____

_____

_____

_____

_____

_____

_____

_____

_____

_____

_____

_____

_____

_____

_____

_____

_____

_____

_____

_____

_____

CHAPTER THREE

# Hidden Treasure #3:
# Talents Over Trials

I was in my office at the church one night when our worship director came in to talk to me about our Christmas program. All of a sudden, in the middle of the conversation, she started to scream—one of those blood-curdling screams you might hear in a horror movie.

I stared at her in shock. What was going on? Had she lost her mind? And then I realized she was looking out the sliding glass door.

I slowly turned so that I could see what she was seeing. There was a man standing outside in the darkness, just staring at us.

I must've jumped about forty feet in the air. After I calmed down—and took a close look at his hands to make sure he wasn't holding any weapons—I opened the sliding glass door and asked the man who he was and what he was doing there.

He replied, "There's hammering and loud music coming from the church, and it's much too noisy."

The man said this as nonchalantly as if he had come up and knocked on the front door of the church to make his complaint instead of creepily lurking outside the back door of my office.

I told him that he could've at least knocked on the back door to let us know he was there. "I did knock," he said.

No, he didn't. He stood there in the dark and stared at us menacingly like he was Michael Myers or Jason or someone, and he scared us half to death.

Anyway, I introduced myself as the pastor and walked him through to the front of the church so I could listen to his complaint. He was friendly and polite about it. When he had finished, I wished him a good evening and he went on his way.

### *A Q&A Session with Jesus*

It was one of those experiences where fear tried to creep its way in and hijack the situation. I mean, it makes perfect sense to be afraid of a shadowy figure lurking outside your office. That's a matter of safety and self-preservation. But once I found out who this man was and why he was there, the fear immediately evaporated.

How many other situations in our lives are hijacked by fear? One year, for Annette's birthday, our daughter bought her a journal. The cover reads, "Let your faith be bigger than your fear."

My daughter gave my wife that birthday gift right while we were in the middle of the rollercoaster ride of doctors' appointments and medical tests that led up to my cancer diagnosis. Talk about God's perfect timing.

The night I received that fateful phone call, I expected to have difficulty sleeping. I anticipated lots of tossing and turning and fear and anxiety over what might happen. But I fell into a deep sleep almost immediately.

Sometimes the Lord will wake me up in the middle of the night to have a conversation, and that night was no exception. He woke me up at about three in the morning, and boy, was I excited to hear from Him in the midst of all of this.

There is a definite difference between waking up on your own and God waking you up. You just know it's Him. If this has happened to you, you know what an awesome experience this is. And if it hasn't, pay attention the next time you wake up in the middle of the night. Ask God if there's something He wants to talk to you about.

In Scripture and also in my own experience, Jesus doesn't just speak to people directly. He also asks questions. That night, He began our conversation by asking me this question: "What is your greatest fear?"

"My greatest fear," I told Him, "is that people will either lose or doubt their faith if they are believers, or that nonbelievers will not believe because they are questioning why a person like me—a pastor—gets sick."

Pastors often get asked tough questions, like, "Why do bad things happen to good people?" I get asked that question a lot. And in many people's eyes, a pastor is the epitome of a good person. So, my greatest fear was that when people found out I had cancer—whether they were believers or nonbelievers—the news would result in them losing or doubting their own faith and the goodness of God.

Instead of interacting with me about my answer to His question, Jesus asked me another question: "How would you live life differently if today were your last day?"

"I would tell people I loved them more," I replied. "I would tell more people about You. I would increase my boldness, and I would ask people to increase their boldness for Your purposes. I would lead unapologetically because I am unapologetically in love."

I was writing those responses down in my journal rather than having a verbal conversation with the Lord—after all, I didn't want to wake up my wife—and I realized I wasn't sure if "unapologetically" was a word.

I googled it to make sure, and a Kelsea Ballerini song called "Unapologetically" popped up in my search results. The lyrics describe an all-in kind of love that doesn't hold back, regardless of where it might lead you.[25]

This is my love for Christ, and this is Christ's love for me. And this is Christ's love for you. He does not apologize for loving us. This is who He is. This is how He rolls. And He is asking us to be unapologetically in love with Him.

After writing down these lyrics in my journal, I continued to write out my response to Jesus' second question: "How would you live life differently if today were your last day?"

"I will hold my wife more. I will tell my children, Sierra and Cayden, how proud I am of them. I will thank my mom and dad for their love for me and tell them how grateful I am for them. I will read my Bible for more wisdom and encouragement."

As soon as I finished writing my response, Jesus engaged with me again—and not with a question this time. He said, "So do that."

He then added, "I'm doing something new in you. I'm purifying your body and your soul so that your spirit can shine even brighter."

"Okay, Lord," I said. "I receive that. I accept that. If You're going to promise me that, then amen."

So, I made a promise back to God: "I will produce more fruit while fully armored."

## *Fear Restricts Us*

We want to give our fear to the Lord, but we want to hold onto our answer to the second question. Our response to how we would live life differently if today were our last day should remind us of how we would really like to live our lives and influence how we live going forward.

When we realize that our lives are changing and the path forward is uncertain, a lot of fear tends to accompany that. And fear can keep us from living the fruitful and abundant lives God intends us to live.

We see fear in action, and how it hinders and binds, in the Parable of the Talents in Matthew 25:14–18 (ESV):

> *For it will be like a man going on a journey, who called his servants and entrusted to them his property. To one he gave five talents, to another two, to another one, to each according to his ability. Then he went away. He who had*

*received the five talents went at once and traded with them, and he made five talents more. So also he who had the two talents made two talents more. But he who had received the one talent went and dug in the ground and hid his master's money.*

At first glance, this passage may seem to be about money, but it is not about money. I love how the English Standard Version uses the word *talent*. In biblical times, one talent was equivalent to 10,000 gold shekels.[26]

So, the master gave 50,000 gold shekels to one servant, and the servant took those talents and made another 50,000. He then gave all ten talents back to his master.

The servant who had been given 20,000 gold shekels made another 20,000, and he too gave all four talents back to his master.

But the servant who received one talent, or 10,000 gold shekels, took his money and buried it in the ground. He was too afraid to do anything with it, so he hid it. As a result, the servant earned nothing—not even interest—and he was thrown out:

*So take the talent from him and give it to him who has the ten talents. For to everyone who has will more be given, and he will have an abundance. But from the one who has not, even what he has will be taken away. And cast the worthless servant into the outer darkness. In that place there will be weeping and gnashing of teeth.*
*—Matthew 25:28–30*

In applying this passage to our own lives, it helps to think of the talents as what we would consider talents—

the gifts and abilities God has given us—rather than a specific amount of money.

Each one of us is uniquely designed with amazing talents, and God is calling us to invest those talents in His kingdom, in His church, and in the lives of others. When we do, we will see Him multiply those talents with incredible results.

It doesn't matter if we have cancer or another chronic disease. We can still contribute to God's kingdom, and we can still experience the abundant and fruitful life God has for us. Each and every one of us has the capacity to bless others with what God has given us, no matter our current challenges. Don't let fear—of an unknown future or of anything else—keep you from investing your talents.

## *Conquering Fear*

God wants us to let go of our fear, receive Him, and then share Him with other people so that we can see a return on that investment. The best way to do this is to defeat the fear and the doubt that come into our lives, and we do so by putting on the armor of God (Ephesians 6:10–17). We'll discuss this in more detail in the next chapter.

The weapon I find myself using the most is the sword of the Spirit, which is the Word of God (Ephesians 6:17). The sword of the Spirit can wipe out any fear that you might have.

Here are seven of my favorite Bible verses for you to meditate on, related to conquering fear:

1. "Peace I leave with you; my peace I give you; I do not give to you as the world gives. Do not let your hearts be troubled and do not be afraid" (John 14:27).

2. "Have I not commanded you? Be strong and courageous. Do not be afraid; do not be discouraged, for the LORD your God will be with you wherever you go" (Joshua 1:9).

3. "Therefore do not worry about tomorrow, for tomorrow will worry about itself. Each day has enough trouble of its own" (Matthew 6:34).

4. "Even though I walk through the darkest valley, I will fear no evil, for you are with me; your rod and your staff, they comfort me" (Psalm 23:4).

5. "I sought the LORD, and he answered me; he delivered me from all my fears" (Psalm 34:4).

6. "The LORD is my light and my salvation—whom shall I fear? The LORD is the stronghold of my life—of whom shall I be afraid?" (Psalm 27:1).

7. "So do not fear, for I am with you; do not be dismayed, for I am your God. I will strengthen you and help you; I will uphold you with my righteous right hand" (Isaiah 41:10).

We can take our greatest fears, leave them at the foot of the cross, and replace them with the confidence God gives us through these promises in His Word.

And when we do, we will see God take our fear and give us faith. Without fear, we are free to live our lives as though today is our last day. We are free to invest our talents as God guides us and watch in amazement as He multiplies our investment.

# Chapter Three Homework

**Question:** What is your greatest fear in regard to your chronic disease or the chronic disease of your loved one? Ask God what He wants to speak to you in response to that fear.

_____

_____

_____

_____

_____

_____

_____

_____

_____

**Question:** How would you live life differently if today were your last day?

_____

_____

_____

_____

_____

_____

_____

_____

_____

_____

**Action:** What talents has God given you? How can you start investing them in His kingdom, in His church, and in the lives of others? Pick one thing this week you can do to take a step toward utilizing your talent.

# *Chapter Three Notes*

CHAPTER FOUR

# Hidden Treasure #4:
# Intimacy in the Challenge

After I received my cancer diagnosis, my level of intimacy with the Lord grew exponentially over a very short period of time. I had thought my relationship with God was pretty good before the diagnosis, but it's grown by leaps and bounds since then.

In fact, I've experienced greater intimacy in all my relationships—with my wife, with my children, with my staff members, with my church, with my lifelong friends.

Several years ago, God gave me a prophetic word. He promised that He would use me to have a global impact on sharing the gospel. At the time, I thought it applied to a particular ministry I was running, but after I received my diagnosis, the Lord slowly unpacked the word "global" for me and revealed how that would happen.

## *Sharing My Diagnosis*

Social media is a powerful tool. It can be used for God's glory, but it can also be used to spread lies, false information, and bad news, causing people to become jaded and skeptical. This makes it difficult for people to see how God is at work on social media platforms.

Annette and I decided to use social media to share what was going on in our lives and in my body. We didn't do it to get a record number of likes or to see how many comments we would get or anything like that.

But as I have read through all the love and support that have been shown to me by people I've known all my life, people I've just met recently, and people I don't know at all, I have been amazed at the ways in which God is using this platform. My social media account is doing what it's supposed to be doing. It's shining light into dark places, and that is an incredible thing to see.

My phone has been ringing off the hook, and I've been getting a ton of text messages. One message was from a friend from college, someone who knew me B.C.—before Christ.

Out of all the text messages I've received, this one might be my favorite, because it came from a very dear friend:

> Jerkoff, I just woke up. Haven't been feeling well. Flu? Anyway, WTF, WTF, WTF. Reading Facebook today gave me a big punch in the gut. Tried calling you, got your voicemail. Called Tom, got an even bigger punch in the gut as he spoke to you a day or two ago. I'm not going to sit here and blow smoke up your #@%. There's only one

thing to do. You need to treat this ^&*# just like you treat everything else in your life—head on. You hear me, meathead? Head #@^%ing on. Micromanage this thing. Learn all you can about it. Do whatever you need to do. Put your $%@#& crying to the side and lean on your friends and your family heavily if you need to. If you need anything whatsoever, I will help. If you need money, hit me up in a pinch. Don't be a &#^%off. Email me or call me or text me, whatever, and I will help in any way I can. I'm not gonna sit here and tell you that I'm gonna pray for you. I don't have your connections in that area. You don't need me for that anyway. Just put your big-boy panties on and tackle this #@%$. And while they're in there fixing things, see if they can do something about your face. That's the real problem. All kidding aside, I'm hurting for you right now. You're a good man, a better husband, and clearly a fantastic father. I LOVE YOU LIKE A BROTHER. Always did. Distance will never change that. Now get off your #$%&ing #$% like I told you before and get in there and kick it. And if you want, I can post this to Facebook with pretty smiley faces and emojis. LOL.

Edited-out f-bombs aside, this is one of the most beautiful text messages I've ever received. When I showed it to my wife, she started laughing, and then she started crying, because she saw the beauty in it, too. We both see this situation as an opportunity to share the love of Christ in a way that most people don't hear about Christ.

Most people hear about Christ not through love, not through connection, not through family. They hear about Christ through media, like stories about the picketing of an abortion clinic or the perceived lack of love for the LGBTQ community, people of other religions, or non-believers.

And more often than not, folks don't fully understand that following Jesus means living a life that models His love of others. Christians have an opportunity and an obligation to help set the record straight by loving our neighbors the way Christ loves us.

If the Lord is going to increase my intimacy with Him and with all these other people whom I love dearly, I say yes to that. I say no to cancer in the name of Jesus, but I say yes to the ways in which He is going to use this situation to better reflect who He truly is and how He truly wants the world to see Him. God is love. God loves you no matter what!

## *Fighting the Cancer Bully*

As I have been thinking about these things, I've realized the Lord has absolutely equipped me to do this well. I've looked back on my life, and parts of it have definitely been a train wreck. I did a lot of crazy things before I said yes to Jesus.

And then He put me on the fast track to being a pastor. I've never asked God why He allowed me to get cancer, but I've certainly asked Him why He called me to be a pastor. That's just nuts.

But there are reasons God has allowed me to have cancer. One of the reasons is that He has taught me how to fight. He has taught me how to fight through wellness and nutrition, as seen in the dietary changes I discussed in Chapter Two. He has also equipped me spiritually to deal with this, which I think is the coolest part.

I love martial arts. I practiced them growing up, and in college, I took a course called "Concepts and Performance of Combat." Over the course of the semester, they taught us all the different styles of martial arts from around the world.

In Japan, for example, one of the main forms of martial arts is karate, which is very straight and linear. If you punch, it's usually in a straight line. The same is true for kicking. In Korea, it's taekwondo. That's all about power. We actually learned how to kick someone through a brick wall. And in China, it's kung fu, which is circular rather than linear. It's very fluid, almost like dancing.

As I was thinking about all of this and the ways in which I understand the martial arts, I asked the Lord how He wanted me to go about my battle with cancer.

He replied, "Sometimes circular and sometimes linear." I immediately knew what He meant.

If you know anything about bullies, they want to provoke you and get you to engage. My bully is cancer, and it wants to provoke and engage. Cancer wants me to make impatient and rash decisions. However, you can defuse a bully by responding to them in a way that is disarming and not antagonistic.

In my teenage years, I took a class in American Kenpo, which combines both circular and linear movements. If someone throws a punch at you, you just step to the side and let their energy flow by you. As you step to the side, you punch them in the groin. You don't even need much power because you're using their own energy against them.

I've taken a similar stance with cancer. Sometimes, I let the words of my doctors fly right by me because I can see the detrimental impact they have on my soul. I've learned that the cancer industry is in the business of provoking.

Not just in my case, but with many of my dear friends who have been diagnosed with cancer, their doctors wanted to rush them into treatment immediately. I hear horror stories, like my own, where doctors use fear as their first line of communication. In my humble opinion, doctors should share truthful information about cancer with different treatment options, and then allow the patient to go home, research for themselves, and process the next best steps moving forward. Unfortunately many patients are so scared of the news their doctor just told them that they blindly jump into treatment without researching for themselves, getting multiple opinions from other experts in the field, or trusting their gut and God.

It makes me think about Jesus. Was He a martial artist? Kind of, because of how He lived His life. I love the ways in which He provided an example of how to communicate well. Sometimes He did it very linearly, and sometimes He was a bit more circular by allowing the power of God to do His work.

A linear example is often found when Jesus was teaching truth to religious leaders. Jesus did not put up with their attempts to trap him in His own words. Instead, Jesus took a direct shot at His bullies:

> *You brood of vipers! How can you speak good, when you are evil? For out of the abundance of the heart the mouth speaks. The good person out of his good treasure brings forth good, and the evil person out of his evil treasure brings forth evil.*
> **—Matthew 12:34–35** (ESV)

A circular example is when we see the power of God flowing through Jesus. In this passage, a distressed woman was bullied by a condition that had been plaguing her for over a decade. Pay attention to how the power of God that flowed through Jesus was enough to heal this woman from her infirmity.

*As Jesus was on his way, the crowds almost crushed him. And a woman was there who had been subject to bleeding for twelve years, but no one could heal her. She came up behind him and touched the edge of his cloak, and immediately her bleeding stopped.*

*"Who touched me?" Jesus asked.*

*When they all denied it, Peter said, "Master, the people are crowding and pressing against you."*

*But Jesus said, "Someone touched me; I know that power has gone out from me."*

*Then the woman, seeing that she could not go unnoticed, came trembling and fell at his feet. In the presence of all the people, she told why she had touched him and how she had been instantly healed. Then he said to her, "Daughter, your faith has healed you. Go in peace."*

**—Luke 8:42b–48**

In my own life, Jesus has corrected me with truth when I have turned my back on him as well as blessed me with His amazing grace and mercy when I exercise faith. Allow the Lord to work in you.

## *A Christian Approach to Basketball*

On the day that we definitively found out that I had cancer, Annette and I went to watch our daughter play basketball. My daughter has been playing basketball since she was five-years old in various independent leagues, and now she was playing for her school league.

She was ten years old at the time, and most of the other ten-year-olds she was playing with had never played basketball before. So she was the one person on the court who knew exactly how to play the game, which was pretty entertaining to watch.

Among the things I love most about my daughter are her brain and her heart. She started the game by focusing on scoring, which wasn't hard for her to do since she could out-dribble every player on the opposing team. But once her team had the lead, she backed off.

My daughter then started passing the ball to every single player on her team until each girl made a basket. She didn't take another shot herself unless the other team scored. Then, she would make baskets until her team was in the lead again and resume her project.

The coaches didn't tell her to do this. This is just how she's wired.

The other thing I found fascinating about my daughter's approach to basketball was that she wouldn't let the other team score at all. Not only was she a more skilled player, but she was also about a head taller than most of the girls. They didn't stand a chance.

She was defending so that her team was protected, and the other team couldn't score. I tried to get her attention from the sidelines and remind her that this was a developmental league and maybe she should let the other team make a few baskets, but she wasn't having it.

I started asking myself, "Why isn't she listening to me?" Then it hit me: it's the Christian thing to do.

My daughter was distributing the ball beautifully among her teammates. It reminded me of how Jesus has access to all the power anyone could ever need, and yet He distributes it among us believers. He gives it to others who need it.

Consider, for example, when Jesus sent out seventy-two of His disciples in Luke 10. He gave them the power to do everything that He had been doing—healing the sick, casting out demons, preaching the gospel.

And when the other team scored, my daughter went in and took the shot. The world tried to score against Jesus, and what did Jesus do? He died on the cross. He won. There was no way He was going to let the enemy win. Jesus was determined to go to the cross for us no matter what and to defend us at all costs.

This is what was going through my head as my daughter was out there on the court, protecting her team. The other team had no chance. She was doing it the way Jesus did it for us.

## *Safety in the Storm*

Jesus went to the cross and died for you and me so that we are promised safe travel to the other side of the lake, even in the midst of the storm (Mark 4:35–41).

I've been reflecting on this passage quite a bit these days. It's such a beautiful passage because it provides a perfect example of who Jesus is:

> That day when evening came, he said to his disciples, "Let us go over to the other side." Leaving the crowd behind, they took him along, just as he was, in the boat. There were also other boats with him. A furious squall came up, and the waves broke over the boat, so that it was nearly swamped. Jesus was in the stern, sleeping on a cushion. The disciples woke him and said to him, "Teacher, don't you care if we drown?"
>
> He got up, rebuked the wind and said to the waves, "Quiet! Be still!" Then the wind died down and it was completely calm.
>
> He said to his disciples, "Why are you so afraid? Do you still have no faith?"
>
> They were terrified and asked each other, "Who is this? Even the wind and the waves obey him!"
> **—Mark 4:35–41**

Jesus has promised us safe travel to the other side of the lake. I am so secure in His arms that He can even take a nap. He's got me, and I'm good.

During your time on planet Earth, you will experience storms. They're inevitable. But Jesus guarantees you safe travel in the midst of them. You can be still and trust Him.

### Keep Calm and Bend Over

At a urology appointment where my doctor was trying to find the source of my cancer, he kept coming up empty-handed. My medical team knew that the cancer was on my hip and up and down my spine, but as I've said previously, they had no idea where it originated.

The urologist was giving it his best effort, though. He had me drop my pants, and he squeezed my family jewels and had me bend over the table so he could check my prostate. Nope, nothing there.

He sat back down in front of his computer and started staring at the screen in hopes of finding something. Annette and I were standing behind him, and I looked at her and burst out laughing.

It was just so amusing to me that the urologist was so confused, but I was calm and still. This dude was freaking out because he couldn't find the source of the cancer, but I already knew the Source. And He is the calm in my storm because I said yes to Him in 2001.

Jesus has shown me what it means to be still and remain quiet in the midst of chaos.

Later that afternoon, I had to come back to the facility so they could stick a camera down my ding-dong. That was not fun, either. As I recover from the PTSD surrounding that experience, I know I can just remain calm. God is good, and He calls us to remain in Him.

## *Get Your Gear On*

God also calls us to stand firm, which makes me think of my daughter out on the basketball court, standing firm for her team.

My daughter wears a uniform when she plays basketball, and God asks us to wear a uniform as well. We need to wear our uniform on a daily basis because we are always in the game. This uniform is described in Ephesians 6:10–20, and it is especially important for us to be reminded of it in the midst of the storm:

> *Finally, be strong in the Lord and in his mighty power. Put on the full armor of God, so that you can take your stand against the devil's schemes. For our struggle is not against flesh and blood, but against the rulers, against the authorities, against the powers of this dark world and against the spiritual forces of evil in the heavenly realms. Therefore put on the full armor of God, so that when the day of evil comes, you may be able to stand your ground, and after you have done everything, to stand. Stand firm then, with the belt of truth buckled around your waist, with the breastplate of righteousness in place, and with your feet fitted with the readiness that comes from the gospel of peace. In addition to all this, take up the shield of faith, with which you can extinguish all the flaming arrows of the evil one. Take the helmet of salvation and the sword of the Spirit, which is the word of God.*
>
> *And pray in the Spirit on all occasions with all kinds of prayers and requests. With this in mind, be alert and always keep on praying for all the Lord's people. Pray also for me, that whenever I speak, words may be given me so that I will fearlessly make known the mystery of the gospel, for which I am an ambassador in chains. Pray that I may declare it fearlessly, as I should.*

Remember, we have really good news. We have the gospel, and more people need to hear about this Jesus, who teaches us how to suit up and teaches us how we can stand firm even in the midst of the battles that we face.

No matter what circumstances we find ourselves in, we have a God who has our back. We have a God who has promised us safe travel to the other side of the lake. In fact, He's taking a nap, and He's calling us to take a nap alongside of Him.

Why should I be afraid of cancer? First John 4:18 tells us that perfect love casts out fear, and I have experienced this perfect love from my family, my friends, my church, and even perfect strangers on social media. I am fearless because I know that I am fearfully and wonderfully made by God Himself (Psalm 139:14).

## *Grow in Intimacy with God*

As Christians, we need to let the world know how we roll. We need to allow the world to see that we handle the storms in our lives differently—and better—than the average Joe because we have been adopted into God's family as sons and daughters.

God has given us these promises, and we are good. We just need to let other people know that.

How do we do this? We increase our intimacy with the Lord. God doesn't care if you're the president of a global ministry or a pastor preaching multiple sermons a day. What He truly cares about is having conversations with His kids.

In Mark 14:36, Jesus referred to God as "Abba, Father." *Abba* is an Aramaic word translated as "Father.[27] Biblical scholars will debate whether or not *Abba* only means "Father," or if it also has a more intimate, childlike translation like "daddy."[28] I'm not here to get into that debate. But I know my personal relationship with Jesus is very intimate, so much so that I refer to Him as Daddy or

Papa when I talk to Him and when I pray to Him. I love it when my kids call me Dad, Papa, Pops, or Daddy, because I know that it reflects a high level of intimacy in our relationship. When I come home from work, Cayden will run to me, shouting, "Daddy! You're home!"

I want to run to my Daddy the same way Cayden runs to me—into His arms, shouting, "Daddy! I'm home!"

We are home. We came home when we said yes to God. He invites everyone to come home, but not everyone accepts that invitation. We have free will, and that's a decision that each of us must make for ourselves.

I made the decision to accept God's invitation in 2001, and my life began to slow down. I began to see things from a different perspective. And I've learned just how important it is to have a deep, intimate, loving relationship with the Lord and to continue to remain calm and stand firm, even in the heat of battle.

When I take my eyes off of Him and start to sink into the lake on which He has called me to walk (Matthew 14:22–33), He reaches His hand out for me and lifts me back up. He helps me to refocus on Him, and we keep moving forward, because He is a God of grace.

And God has used my diagnosis and my close relationship with Him to offer His grace to other people who otherwise might not have had the opportunity to know Him as He desires to be known. To me, that makes my storm worth it. With the Lord's help and equipping, I will remain calm and stand firm until the end.

# Chapter Four Homework

**Question:** Do you think people who observe how you approach life get a glimpse of who God is? How can this situation help you grow to a place where you better reflect who God truly is and how He truly wants the world to see Him?

_____

_____

_____

_____

_____

_____

_____

_____

_____

**Question:** What can you do to practice rest—to take a nap—in your situation? What does that look like for you specifically?

_____

_____

_____

_____

_____

_____

_____

_____

_____

**Action:** Increase your intimacy with the Lord. He wants to have a conversation with you. Set your intentions to converse with God daily and to grow your intimacy with Him. If you haven't accepted God's invitation to come home to Him, reflect on what that would mean for you and consider saying yes to Him.

## *Chapter Four Notes*

_____

_____

_____

_____

_____

_____

_____

_____

_____

_____

_____

_____

_____

_____

_____

_____

_____

_____

_____

_____

_____

_____

CHAPTER FIVE

# Hidden Treasure #5:
# Invite God to Your Pity Party

Have you ever had a pity party? Maybe it was for your-self, or maybe someone else invited you to theirs.

A pity party can be defined as an instance of indulging in self-pity or eliciting pity from other people. I love this more detailed definition from the Urban Dictionary: "A way of experiencing grief in which you spend your time feeling sorry for yourself and whining endlessly over how crappy your life is. Pity parties can be just for one or for many people, such as maybe your friends and close peo-ple, who will try to comfort you or just be there for you while you keep asking yourself what did you do to deserve whatever it is that made you so sad in the first place."[29]

I have definitely thrown a pity party or two for myself since I was diagnosed with terminal cancer. On one occa-sion, my pity party coincided with a pity party my wife was throwing for herself. Usually, we offset each other's pity parties: one of us will be down in the dumps, and the other will be able to reassure them and tell them everything's going to be okay.

On this particular day, though, both of us were on a downward spiral. She was out with her friends, and I was attending a birthday party my son was invited to, with a dozen other rambunctious kids (and parents). All I wanted to do was to have a pity party, and they wanted to have a real party. It was hard for me not to be grumpy.

After a long day in which everyone else seemed to be having fun but us, Annette woke me up at three in the morning, and we had a pity party together.

But we decided to make God the guest of honor at our pity party. As we clung to each other in the middle of the night, we invited the goodness of God into our conversation as we shared our personal challenges. We reminded each other of our faith in Him. We reminded each other of His love for us individually and as a couple. We reminded each other of the Bible verse we had chosen for our wedding day: "A cord of three strands is not quickly broken" (Ecclesiastes 4:12). You see, when you invite God to your pity party, the pity part of the party goes away. It's amazing how that happens.

## *Our Good, Good Father*

What's your impression of God during your pity party? For me, I see God as Yoda from the meme where he says, "To the hand you talk, because listening I am not." Sometimes when we're spiraling down, we feel like God has His hand up to us and that He doesn't even want to hear us—but that is not our good Father. Our God is good, and He is good all the time.

God describes Himself in Scripture as a great and compassionate Father who is slow to anger and abounding in love. Consider Psalm 103:8–13:

> The LORD is compassionate and gracious, slow to anger, abounding in love. He will not always accuse, nor will he harbor his anger forever; he does not treat us as our sins deserve or repay us according to our iniquities. For as high as the heavens are above the earth, so great is his love for those who fear him; as far as the east is from the west, so far has he removed our transgressions from us.
>
> As a father has compassion on his children, so the LORD has compassion on those who fear him.

It's important to understand that "fearing the LORD" means to honor Him. When we honor the Lord, He has tremendous compassion on us.

God is not angry. He is in a good mood. Sometimes we have this image of Him as an angry dad because of the experiences we've had with our earthly parents.

Earthly parents screw up sometimes. The other day, I was doing the dishes. My son came into the kitchen, and I just snapped at him. He did nothing wrong. It was all on me, and I realized it almost immediately. I find that my fuse is much shorter when I am dealing with bone pain from this cancer. I feel bad for my family because they are often on the end of my short fuse.

Cayden called me out on my behavior, too, asking, "Dad, why did you just do that to me? I didn't even do anything." I apologized right away and asked his forgiveness.

I've discovered that sometimes, I am quick to anger. But God is a good Father. He is not quick to anger, and He is never going to snap at us. He is compassionate and abounding in love.

James 1:16–18 (MSG) says:

> *So, my very dear friends, don't get thrown off course. Every desirable and beneficial gift comes out of heaven. The gifts are rivers of light cascading down from the Father of Light. There is nothing deceitful in God, nothing two-faced, nothing fickle. He brought us to life using the true Word, showing us off as the crown of all his creatures.*

What a beautiful description of God showing us how much He loves us. When He looks at us, He sees the crown of everything He has created.

Psalm 119:68–72 (NLT) says:

> *You are good and do only good; teach me your decrees. Arrogant people smear me with lies, but in truth I obey your commandments with all my heart. Their hearts are dull and stupid, but I delight in your instructions. My suffering was good for me, for it taught me to pay attention to your decrees. Your instructions are more valuable to me than millions in gold and silver.*

I can get all caught up in my pity party and my cancer pain, but when I'm focused on God, I realize that He is doing something amazing in me and through me. He is showing me just how much love He has for me and why He has allowed these circumstances in my life.

God's love is abundant and overflowing. It's not something I'm trying to hold onto with my fingertips; I'm hugging it. I'm hugging God, and I'm thanking Him because I know He's got this. I know He's got me. And I've got nothing to fear because He is a good Father.

## *God Is Trustworthy*

Because God is a good Father, we can trust Him regardless of our current circumstances. No matter how unpleasant our situation may be or how horrible the season is that we are going through, we can always, always trust in the Lord.

Romans 8:28–32 (NLT) reminds us:

*And we know that God causes everything to work together for the good of those who love God and are called according to his purpose for them. For God knew his people in advance, and he chose them to become like his Son, so that his Son would be the firstborn among many brothers and sisters. And having chosen them, he called them to come to him. And having called them, he gave them right standing with himself. And having given them right standing, he gave them his glory.*

*What shall we say about such wonderful things as these? If God is for us, who can ever be against us? Since he did not spare even his own Son but gave him up for us all, won't he also give us everything else?*

God gave us His Son, Jesus, who died on the cross for our sins. He gave us that kind of love and defeated death for us, and with Jesus now in glory, God is also giving that glory to us. Isn't that a good Father? Isn't that a God we can trust regardless of our circumstances?

James 1:17–18 (NLT) says:

> *Whatever is good and perfect is a gift coming down to us from God our Father, who created all the lights in the heavens. He never changes or casts a shifting shadow. He chose to give birth to us by giving us his true word. And we, out of all creation, became his prized possession.*

Sometimes, circumstances just suck (like the Dodgers). And yet, God calls us His children and His prized possession, and He has promised us the crown of life if we will patiently endure our seasons of testing. We can trust Him in everything.

## *Jesus Displays the Goodness of God*

Have you ever thought to yourself something along the lines of *there is absolutely no way God would ever forgive me for what I've done?* I have. In fact, I could write another multi-chapter book on the things I've done wrong and the people I have hurt in this lifetime. But when Jesus displays his goodness, and the lessons He wants us to learn, we get a much deeper understanding of the love and forgiveness He desires us to embrace.

One of my favorite examples of this is the woman caught in adultery found in John 8:1–11. The teachers of the law and the Pharisees were wanting to stone her.

Instead of Jesus picking up a rock, rousing up the crowd, and chucking it at this woman's head, He used this teaching moment for both the individual and the group. This poor woman, who was about to be stoned to death, not only received the grace and mercy from Jesus, but she saw that she was not alone in her mistakes. Each person dropped their rocks, as they realize that they too were not in the position to judge this woman.

Those in the crowd with the most years behind them, were also the first to drop their stones. If you are reading this book and are as old or older than me, you know exactly what was going on in the minds of the first to drop their stones. Jesus knew this too as He watched the crowd disperse. I can image myself, at this scene, dropping my rock realizing that it is not my place to judge someone else's sin when I too need a clean record.

I challenge you to make the ultimate forgiver of sins, Jesus, the guest of honor in your life—in every circumstance, in every decision, in every interaction, and at every pity party, invite Him in.

# Chapter Five Homework

**Question:** Have you indulged in a pity party since the diagnosis of your chronic disease or the chronic disease of your loved one? How does settling into a pity party affect you overall? How does it affect your relationship with God? How could it look if you were to invite God into your pity party?

_____

_____

_____

_____

_____

_____

_____

_____

_____

_____

**Question:** What's your impression of God during your pity parties? What specific Bible verses can you recall to help you return to a truthful perspective of who God is, during those times when you are struggling to see that He is good?

_____

_____

_____

_____

_____

_____

_____

_____

_____

_____

**Action:** Invite Jesus to be the guest of honor in your life and in your circumstances. In a notebook or journal, record the difference He makes when you engage with Him in those places of pity, fear, and doubt.

## *Chapter Five Notes*

_____

_____

_____

_____

_____

_____

_____

_____

_____

_____

_____

_____

_____

_____

_____

_____

_____

_____

_____

_____

_____

_____

_____

_____

CHAPTER SIX

# Hidden Treasure # 6:
# Healing Body and Mind

I love the game of golf. As my cancer progresses, I find that I am mourning the loss of things that I can no longer do. I try not to allow the pity party bug to enter my brain because if I do, I will forget that our time here is only temporary and there are most likely some amazing golf courses in eternity. In the meantime, I will continue to pray for a miracle that God will heal my body and get me back on the greens.

God's peace surpasses all understanding (Philippians 4:7). In the midst of that peace, He has been helping us to receive all this bad news with a hearty dose of humor. Sometimes the news is so ridiculously bad, all Annette and I can do is laugh.

## *Cutting off Goliath's Head*

I decided to have genomic DNA testing done to see what other options I might have for treating my cancer. This type of testing looks at the mutations that are happening at the DNA level, which helps them to determine how to best treat the disease.

I received a twenty-three-page report on these four different types of mutations they found inside my body and what treatment protocols they would recommend. And when I walked into my oncologist's office with that report, I felt like David carrying the head of Goliath, the giant he had just slain, to Jerusalem in victory.

Here's the report's summary statement: "There are no approved therapies in this patient's tumor type that are specific to the reported genomic alterations." Let me translate that for you: "There is no cure for what you have."

You see, David was confused by the Israelites' lack of faith. David knew he had God on his side. He was not afraid of this giant. We too were well equipped spiritually to deal with whatever the oncologist said because we already knew the bad news and had the time to process. We also knew that no matter the circumstances, we had God on our side.

Annette is a whiz at research. She's an excellent student and extremely knowledgeable, so there wasn't anything the oncologist could say that could surprise us. No matter what came out of the doctor's mouth, we would be good.

The oncologist came in, and for legal reasons, she had to explain everything to us in terms of the worst-case scenario. She told us, with sadness in her face, that I probably only had two years left to live, even with treatment.

Maybe she didn't realize that it's not her call to determine my last day. She didn't understand we were approaching this from a posture of victory rather than defeat.

We lovingly told the oncologist that we were praying for her and that it was going to be all right, which was a bit strange. Doesn't the doctor normally comfort the patient? We told her there was going to be an opportunity for her to learn something as she observed us and how we navigated this diagnosis.

I asked the oncologist what her take was on healthy eating and physical activity. She kind of brushed off the question. She never once suggested that I try any treatment method other than what was FDA approved. Apparently, the Food and Drug Administration only focuses on the drugs and not the food? That's fine—I understood that she had to do things a certain way, and she recommended two intense chemotherapies.

I'm not against chemotherapy, radiation, surgery, or any other standard cancer treatments. If the doctors had been able to locate the source of my cancer and put together a plan involving those treatments, I might have actually given them the okay. I just wish they were also allowed to color outside the lines.

They didn't have a solution, so we got to discover our own path, our own treasures.

## *Pounced On by the Lord's Presence*

Before that fateful oncology appointment, I visited a church that has amazing testimonies of healings happening all the time, and I asked them to pray over me for healing. While one of their prayer teams was standing around me and praying for me, they asked me if I felt anything.

I didn't really feel anything apart from generally feeling good. I told them that the only way I'd know if their prayers had been answered would be to have some tests done.

As I was telling them that, my legs started to wobble, which was unusual for me. All of a sudden—*boom!* I was face down on the ground, and the Lord's presence landed on top of me.

The prayer team knew from experience that I was going to be there for a while, so they covered me with a blanket and moved on to the next person who needed prayer.

While I was down on the ground, the Lord gave me a beautiful vision of my son, Cayden, at age 18. We were playing golf in Ireland together. I pray continuously that this was a prophetic vision and that in just a few short years, Cayden and I will be killing golf balls in Killarney. That, of course, is up to God, and I leave it in His mighty hands.

## *A Picture of Complete Health*

Jesus is calling us to get our bodies into an optimal state of health, one that encompasses our entire person. Let's take a look at 1 Thessalonians 5:16–24:

> *Rejoice always, pray continually, give thanks in all circumstances; for this is God's will for you in Christ Jesus.*
>
> *Do not quench the Spirit. Do not treat prophecies with contempt but test them all; hold on to what is good, reject every kind of evil.*
>
> *May God himself, the God of peace, sanctify you through and through. May your whole spirit, soul and body be kept blameless at the coming of our Lord Jesus Christ. The one who calls you is faithful, and he will do it.*

This is a great passage for us to hold onto because it gives us a road map for whole-person healthy living.

We are called to rejoice always (1 Thessalonians 5:16), even when we're in the midst of difficult circumstances, and to always be in conversation with God through prayer (1 Thessalonians 5:17)—not just when we feel like it or when we need something.

Get yourself into the mindset of having a continuous conversation with your Creator. Talk to Him when you're driving to work or doing chores around the house.

Before this diagnosis, these passages weren't even on my radar. Now I'm praising God and thanking Him for what He's doing and about to do.

This passage then warns us not to quench the Spirit (1 Thessalonians 5:19). I have been to churches where it is very obvious that the Holy Spirit is being squelched, and it is not a pretty sight. We need to allow the Holy Spirit to flow through us freely and unfettered.

We are also to exercise discernment in regard to prophecies (1 Thessalonians 5:20–21). Someone might tell you that God has given them a word for you, and you need to make sure you test what God has supposedly told them to tell you. Sometimes a person might tell you something they think they heard from the Lord, but it isn't really from the Lord. It's their own thoughts and opinions, or their own issues that they're projecting onto you, and you need to protect yourself from that. You need to test the prophetic words that are being spoken into you.

I do this by calling other brothers and sisters in the Lord whom I trust, sharing the prophetic word with them, and asking what they think. They might respond with a prophetic word of their own that confirms it, or they might tell me they're seeing something different. That's how God works—but you have to test it out.

I ask other people about the visions and prophecies I receive as well, like the vision I received about playing golf with my son when he's eighteen years old. It's important to ask and check and test. As we do so, God will refine our discernment and guide us on the right path.

We are to reject every kind of evil (1 Thessalonians 5:22). If something in particular is coming to mind as you read that, pay attention to it, and then run it by someone to test it. God may be revealing to you what that verse means for you.

God Himself, the God of peace, will then sanctify us through and through (1 Thessalonians 5:23). He won't only sanctify our mind or our body—He will sanctify everything, every part of us. He will continue to refine us so that we better reflect His goodness.

The Lord will be faithful to keep our entire spirit, soul, and body blameless at His coming (1 Thessalonians 5:23–24). He will do it, and we can trust Him.

## *Power Washing My Life*

God is sanctifying us from the inside out. He is doing that to me spiritually, and He is also doing it physically through my diet of fruits and vegetables. It's not just about my spirit but about my body and my soul as well, and He is exposing things in all three areas that I shouldn't be doing.

It's like a comprehensive power-wash, and I desperately need it. We all need it, and God is willing to do that for each and every one of us. By submitting to this process of refining and sanctification, we will be able to bless others, because our cup will be clean both inside and out and overflowing with His goodness.

When the doctor told me I only had two years left to live, I wondered how she could be so certain. After all, it's not like how long I live is up to her. That's up to God. When He does call me home, hallelujah! That's a win-win situation.

## *Psychoneuroimmunology and You*

The study of the relationship between the mind and the body is known as psychoneuroimmunology. This branch of science addresses "the influence of emotional states (such as stress) and nervous system activities on immune function especially in relation to the onset and progression of disease."[30] In a nutshell, psychoneuroimmunology is the study of the mind–body connection. It's a relatively new branch of medicine.

The immune system has an amazing ability to fight off attackers. Think of your immune system as a seedy bar where a fight is getting underway. In a bar like that, there are always a couple of creepy guys hanging out around the pool table. You know the guys I'm talking about. They give you a bad feeling as soon as you walk through the door. You just know they're going to be trouble.

Well, your immune system feels the same away about any germs that enter your body, and it sets off a response that creates the antibodies you need to fight off the germs. The way our body produces these antibodies is through our B cells.[31]

B cells circulate throughout our body, just waiting for a germ to try to start something. There are two types of B cells: plasma cells and memory cells. The plasma B cells will surround the germs and start attacking them. The memory B cells then come in and basically record how the attack was conducted so that the plasma B cells can launch the same attack if another germ of that type enters the body.

The body also releases T cells as part of the immune response. There are different types of T cells, including memory T cells. My favorite type of T cells are the cytotoxic T cells, or killer T cells, because they look like Shrek. We also have suppressor T cells, which shut down the body's immune response once the threat has been taken care of. Without the suppressor T cells, the immune system will start attacking healthy cells after it's finished attacking all the germs.

## The Remedy for Stress

What's interesting about this mind–body–emotion relationship is that our mind often suppresses the immune response. If your mind is out of whack and then you get stressed out on top of that, you might end up getting sick. There are three ways we can remedy this issue.

1.  As we discussed earlier in the book, we can boost our immune system through better nutrition. If we eat God's foods, foods that grow from the ground, it increases our immune response and helps us to get our B cells and our T cells in a healthy balance.

2.  We can also turn to brothers and sisters in Christ whom we love and trust and ask them to support us in prayer.

3.  Most importantly, however, we can turn to the Word of God and ask the Lord for His help in managing our stress. As Proverbs 17:22 teaches us, "A cheerful heart is good medicine, but a crushed spirit dries up the bones."

Our emotions have an impact on our immune system, and we can improve our emotional state by spending time in the Word of God and meditating on God's goodness.

One of my favorite passages to meditate on is Matthew 11:28–30: "Come to me, all you who are weary and burdened, and I will give you rest. Take my yoke upon you and learn from me, for I am gentle and humble in heart, and you will find rest for your souls. For my yoke is easy and my burden is light."

This was Jesus Himself speaking to His followers, and He was saying, "When you're worried, come to Me. I will give you rest."

Another great passage to meditate on when you're feeling stressed is John 14:27: "Peace I leave with you; my peace I give you. I do not give to you as the world gives. Do not let your hearts be troubled and do not be afraid."

The Lord has given us His peace! Everyday life is full of distractions. We need to take time out of our busy lives to rest in His presence and be filled once again with His peace. Sometimes you need to find a quiet, peaceful place where you can go into that hidden place in your soul and spend time with the Lord.

When we find ourselves in stressful circumstances, we can turn to Him. If we're constantly caught up in the rat race, we're not giving ourselves the bandwidth to receive the peace that God wants to give us so that we can have a healthy mind.

Psalm 55:22 reminds us, "Cast your cares on the LORD and he will sustain you; he will never let the righteous be shaken." This verse makes it very clear that if we cast our cares on the Lord, He sustains us. Sometimes we try to white-knuckle our way through life and do everything ourselves. That's not how God rolls. He's asking us to let it go and hand it over to Him, because we don't need excessive worry in our lives.

## *Humility: A Key Ingredient in Mental Health*

First Peter 5:6–8 also talks about casting our burdens on the Lord: "Humble yourselves, therefore, under God's mighty hand, that he may lift you up in due time. Cast all your anxiety on him because he cares for you. Be alert and of sober mind. Your enemy the devil prowls around like a roaring lion looking for someone to devour."

Humbling ourselves is a tough thing to do. I know I have trouble with that sometimes. However, it's important for me to be able to say to the Lord, "This is not about me, this is about everything else that is trying to attack my life, and I need to submit myself to You fully and completely."

I had an experience where I needed to humble myself after receiving a phone call from a friend whose father had suddenly passed away from a stroke at a young age. This friend and his wife also happened to be the first couple I had the blessing to marry, and that experience contributed to my decision to become a pastor. These were dear friends of ours, and I knew his parents well.

I was extremely upset by the news at first. This man was such a great father and grandfather. Why did he have to die at such a young age? The more I sat and stewed in my anger, the heavier my heart became. I then realized that I needed to humble myself, so I asked the Lord to take the anger from me.

It's healthy for us to mourn and grieve, and there's absolutely nothing wrong with doing that. But I have noticed, when I stay too long in my grief and anger, it sets off a chain reaction. One emotion triggers another emotion, and that emotion might be unhealthy. This ultimately leads to a downward spiral that stresses me out, impacts my immune system, and takes me out completely.

I'm therefore doing my best to get myself to a place of humility where I can say, "Lord, I receive this very sad news, and I need You to help me and guide me through this. I give myself to You. May Your mighty hand lift me up in due time as I cast my anxiety onto You because You care about me."

Our God, the Creator of the universe, cares about us. But the passage then warns us to be alert and of sober mind because the devil is on the prowl, looking for someone to devour. The enemy wants to sneak into our hearts through our sadness and say, "By the way, you're not just sad. You're also a loser"—or anything else that might take us out.

We need to make sure we're protecting ourselves from that by humbling ourselves before God and asking for His help, grace, and protection. The enemy will use our anxiety to get to us, but when we cast our cares on the Lord, he can't touch us.

## *Words Can Help or Hurt*

Proverbs 12:25 tells us, "Anxiety weighs down the heart, but a kind word cheers it up." It's important that we understand the power of our tongue. The tongue has the power to kill, and it also has the power to give life (Proverbs 18:21).

I taught that concept to the students in the team-building class I teach at San Jose State University. It was their first day of class, and I encouraged them to build each other up. They looked at me like I was crazy, but I told them, "Even though you're just meeting each other, you'll soon be forming teams, and the best thing you can do as a team is to build each other up."

We need to pay attention to the words that we're using, because we can either kill someone else or we can build them up. We have to pay close attention to how we communicate with each other and what each individual needs. Someone might need a word of instruction, while someone else might need a word of correction, but that word should always be sandwiched between words of encouragement.

If you only approach someone with the things they need to fix and leave out the growth and encouragement, you are not that great a communicator. Why? Because the person you're talking to will be taken out by your words instead of being built up by them. They won't be able to receive the correction or criticism because it's delivered too harshly.

If you use your words to encourage others, you can actually change their psychoneuroimmunology—by changing the way their heart is receiving words. When a person feels encouraged and built up, it has an impact on their overall health. If you speak life into someone, you will see life. Instead of speaking death into each other, maybe we should try speaking life into each other.

## *Contentment Casts Out Worry*

As a pastor, I often notice another worry that takes people out mentally, emotionally, and physically: concern over money. Hebrews 13:5–6 states, "Keep your lives free from the love of money and be content with what you have, because God has said, 'Never will I leave you; never will I forsake you.' So we say with confidence, 'The Lord is my helper; I will not be afraid. What can mere mortals do to me?'"

Money is one of the biggest and most common stressors. The Bible mentions it several times, including in this passage in Hebrews. We get so worried about whether we'll have enough money for this thing or that thing, and we forget that God provides.

You may be feeling anxious about your finances. But if you cast your worries onto God, you'll be amazed at how your stress evaporates. You'll be able to focus on what you do have instead of what you don't have, and you'll find yourself praising God for everything He's given you. The worries that are trying to take you out will no longer have a deep impact on you because you're praising God rather than complaining.

Fear is a major stressor, too. Stress causes the body to break down, impacts our T cells and our B cells, and completely wipes us out. But Psalm 56:3 says, "When I am afraid, I put my trust in you."

## *Training the Mind*

The Lord is asking us to take the power of His Word and apply it. We do this by training our mind so that His Word becomes part of who we are. His Spirit will flow out of us if we can get our minds to understand and embrace the goodness of God.

It's good to have a healthy body, but we also need to have a healthy mind. Our mind is more than just our brain. It also encompasses our thoughts and our emotions.

So, how do we train our mind? Romans 8:5–8 (ESV) offers us some insight:

> For those who live according to the flesh set their minds on the things of the flesh, but those who live according to the Spirit set their minds on the things of the Spirit. For to set the mind on the flesh is death, but to set the mind on the Spirit is life and peace. For the mind that is set on the flesh is hostile to God, for it does not submit to God's law; indeed, it cannot. Those who are in the flesh cannot please God.

Rather than only being concerned about our own desires and what will make us feel good—how much money we have, how our relationships with other people are benefitting us, etc.—we need to focus on what God's Spirit, who lives inside us, wants. When we are guided by the Spirit, all those other things just fall away. They no longer matter at all.

Once we set our minds on what the Spirit wants us to do, we start living our lives according to the Spirit rather than the flesh. In my college days, I probably lived 110 percent according to the flesh. I didn't have the Spirit living inside me, so the flesh was the only thing I could understand.

But once God got a hold of me and infused me with His Spirit, I realized that He wanted me to pursue Him and not the things of the flesh. Once I started pursuing Him, I realized that all that other stuff didn't even matter anymore.

Keeping our eyes on Jesus results in life and peace. Only caring about the things of the flesh leads to death. When we focus on the Spirit, the Spirit starts to change who we are. We start to drink the living water that comes from the throne of God (Revelation 22:1), and that increases the wellbeing of our mind, body, and soul. Drinking God's water changes everything, and we need to tap into that.

Romans 12:2 tells us, "Do not be conformed to this world, but be transformed by the renewal of your mind, that by testing you may discern what is the will of God, what is good and acceptable and perfect" (ESV).

We need to be transformed by the renewal of our minds, which will then make it possible for us to understand God's will for our lives. Instead of going after the things of the flesh, we are drinking God's living water, and we are better able to discern God's path for us.

Colossians 3:1–4 says:

> Since, then, you have been raised with Christ, set your hearts on things above, where Christ is, seated at the right hand of God. Set your minds on things above, not on earthly things. For you died, and your life is now hidden with Christ in God. When Christ, who is your life, appears, then you also will appear with him in glory.

How amazing is it that we have a God who has not only resurrected Himself but will also resurrect us to be with Him? That is the incredible promise we have received through Jesus' death on the cross and His resurrection. He died so that we, too, can be resurrected to full life.

Our life here on earth is very brief—maybe ninety or a hundred years at the most. It passes by in the blink of an eye. Yet God has given us eternity.

This is the amazing thing about the gospel, and it's something that people need to hear. It breaks my heart when people don't have the hope of eternity. This earthly life has an end, and without that hope, there is nothing at all for them to look forward to.

But in Jesus, that end is only the beginning. We have the promise of eternal life because of what He accomplished on the cross, because of His resurrection. It's the beginning of the story, not the end.

This is what gives us a cheerful heart, and a cheerful heart is good medicine (Proverbs 17:22). We know that death is not the end. In fact, we're just getting started.

## *Life, from Here to Eternity*

If you're hearing about this good news for the first time, I encourage you to simply receive it. All you need to do is say, "Yes, Lord. I believe in You, and I want to follow You. I recognize that I have sinned against You, and I accept that Jesus died on the cross for my sins. I want to drink from Your living water for eternity."

May God pour down His living water upon us so that it soaks us and splashes onto everyone around us so that they can get a taste of His living water as well.

But before we get to eternity, we have a life to finish living here, and it makes that life easier for us and more effective for God's kingdom if we are pursuing a state of optimal health for our bodies and our minds. With God's Word as our guide, we can live our healthiest life possible and help others to do the same.

# Chapter Six Homework

**Question:** Do you live a lifestyle of prayer and thanksgiving? When you sense anxiety stirring, do you turn to the Lord to cast your cares on Him? Write out some words or phrases of life to which you can turn in times of stress and anxiety.

_____

_____

_____

_____

_____

_____

_____

_____

_____

**Question:** Are you allowing God to sanctify you holistically, in mind, body, and spirit? Are certain areas being neglected? What changes can you make?

_____

_____

_____

_____

_____

_____

_____

_____

_____

_____

**Action:** Look at the list of the three ways to remedy stress (diet, community, and the Word of God). Examine whether and how much you are utilizing these remedies in your life. Is there a remedy you can lean into, to better combat stress in your life? If so, take steps forward today to implement that remedy.

# *Chapter Six Notes*

CHAPTER SEVEN

# Hidden Treasure #7:
# A Soul Makeover

*I take you to have and to hold from this day forward, for better or for worse, for richer or for poorer, in sickness and in health, to love and to cherish, till death do us part.*

Dang, when I said those words to Annette on June 21, 2003, I had no idea how challenging it would be to live up to that covenant we made before God and a crowd of witnesses. If you read my dedication letter I wrote to Annette at the end of this book, you may pick up on a prayer request that I made asking God to heal our marriage. I am proud to say God delivered on that prayer request. Praise the Lord.

In just over five years as a lead pastor, I have seen many marriages fall apart. Every one of these marriages (family, friends, church members) that did not work out absolutely broke my heart. I think the main reason is how easily people gave up and gave into the weakness of their own souls. In today's society, married couples forget the words they say on their wedding day and allow the enemy to steal, kill, and destroy. Both men and women are guilty of stinkin' thinkin' and feel that they are right while the other person is wrong. It is all "their fault."

Since my cancer diagnosis, there have been so many times where I would unhinge on poor Annette and blame her for everything wrong in my life. I am willing to bet she might say the same. Cancer really sucks, and besides attempting to go metastatic in my body, it's tried to spread to my marriage as well. Well, F.U. cancer. You can't have my marriage, so get behind me, Satan!

You see, cancer does not just impact the person with the disease. It also impacts the caregiver (and in our case, our children too). Whether you are a spouse, a sibling, a friend, or a child of a sick parent, the disease *will* have a major impact on your wellbeing. I have noticed that cancer has caused my personality to change. I am much more introverted, which in itself is not a bad thing; however, when a disease causes a personality to change in someone you have known and loved for a very long time, as a caregiver you will need to adjust to this new personality. The biggest cause of my change in personality is having to adjust to newfound pain levels in my body.

I have had suicidal thoughts since my diagnosis, and I have been blessed by a great therapist who has helped me with unhealthy feelings. In fact, she is partially responsible for the title of this book, *Hidden Treasures,* which presented itself during one of my therapy sessions.

If you are experiencing suicidal thoughts, please contact the **National Suicide Prevention Lifeline at 800-273-8255 or suicidepreventionlifeline.org**. You may be reading this for the first time: please know that these thoughts are normal for individuals with chronic/terminal disease. Please seek help.

My Bible has taught me to find peace in the middle of the storm. When I am dialed into God, I can also give you examples of when I am completely loving toward my family even when dealing with severe pain or nausea. When my spirit is in alignment with the Holy Spirit, the weakness of my flesh does not win.

## *Healing Our Soul = Healing Our Relationships*

In addition to wanting us to pursue healing for our bodies and our minds, God wants us to pursue healing for our souls. We need to have a good balance between our soul and our spirit. If our soul is stronger than our spirit and starts taking over, it can have a negative impact on our health and the health of our relationships.

Let's start by taking a look at Mark 8:31–33 (ESV):

> *And he began to teach them that the Son of Man must suffer many things and be rejected by the elders and the chief priests and the scribes and be killed, and after three days rise again. And he said this plainly. And Peter took him aside and began to rebuke him. But turning and seeing his disciples, he rebuked Peter and said, "Get behind me, Satan! For you are not setting your mind on the things of God, but on the things of man."*

The last few sentences of that passage really jump out at me. Just prior to this exchange, Peter had identified Jesus as the Messiah, and Jesus had told Peter that he was the rock on which the church would be built (Matthew 16:13–20). And now, Peter was upset with Jesus for talking about His coming death.

Peter was so caught up in his own flesh, in his own desire for Jesus to live, that he told Jesus to stop talking like that. Peter was worried about his friend and didn't want to believe such a thing could be true.

Jesus rebuked him right away, and it's interesting how He rebuked him. He didn't say, "Get behind me, Peter!" He said, "Get behind me, Satan!"

When we allow Satan to get a hold of our anxieties and our worries, they take over and start to control us. We get so caught up in our own selfish desires, ambitions, and insecurities that we forget about the things of God. This is exactly what Jesus was saying to Peter here.

Jesus also recognized that Peter was talking loudly enough, what he was saying could have influenced the people around him. We see this in verse 33 when Jesus turned and saw His disciples while Peter was rebuking Him a short distance from the rest of the group. It's at this point that Jesus rebuked Peter.

The enemy loves to do this to us, by the way. He loves to take out our mind by getting us too engrossed in what we think people are and how we think people should behave, ourselves included. We get caught up in that instead of focusing on the Lord and asking for His will to be done.

Let's move onto Mark 8:34–38 (ESV):

*And calling the crowd to him with his disciples, he said to them, "If anyone would come after me, let him deny himself and take up his cross and follow me. For whoever would save his life will lose it, but whoever loses his life for my sake and the gospel's will save it. For what does it profit a man to gain the whole world and forfeit his soul? For what can a man give in return for his soul? For whoever is ashamed of me and of my words in this adulterous and sinful generation, of him will the Son of Man also be ashamed when he comes in the glory of his Father with the holy angels."*

The crowd and Jesus' disciples had just witnessed Peter pulling Jesus aside to rebuke Him and Jesus rebuking Peter in return, and Jesus now turned and addressed them.

I love what Jesus said in verse 36: "For what does it profit a man to gain the whole world and forfeit his soul?" Why would Jesus give into the temptation of the devil? And Peter shouldn't have done that, either.

I, however, do that all the time. I find myself giving into the devil's schemes to scare me away from the purpose to which God has called me. I also see this in marriages, and in my marriage. The enemy wants to distract my marriage with things like cancer, money, or differences in parenting, or by highlighting my own weaknesses or Annette's weaknesses.

This happens to us today in real time. This isn't just something that happened to Peter two thousand years ago. These lessons apply to us in this very moment because "the word of God is living and active, sharper than any two-edged sword, piercing to the division of soul and of spirit, of joints and of marrow, and discerning the thoughts and intentions of the heart" (Hebrews 4:12 ESV).

## *Defining the Soul*

Jesus' statement about what it would profit a person to give up their soul (Mark 8:36) makes me think about how our soul sometimes controls our lives.

When I think of the soul, I think of a sumo wrestler. If our soul becomes too pumped up, it can overpower other aspects of ourselves. With a healthy soul, our breath, our heart, our desires, our emotions, and our morals are all in alignment with God's will.

Have you noticed that when you're anxious, your breathing becomes very shallow? I have a Fitbit that, among other functions, helps me to control my breathing as I follow along with it. It tells me when to inhale and when to exhale. It's a great tool for managing anxiety.

What happens is that we get so stressed out, we lose our alignment with the Lord. All of sudden, the soul takes over and we start following the ways of the world. We become so anxious that we can't eat or we're on the verge of hyperventilating. These are the results when our soul becomes too powerful in our lives. "It would be so much easier if we just got a divorce." This statement runs through your head more readily than "I am going to do everything I can to assure Annette that I am going to remain true to our wedding vows."

How about you? Divorce is easy; marriage is not. Are you giving in to the weakness of your soul, or are you exercising and strengthen your spirit?

Our breath, our heart, our desires, our emotions, and our morals all get out of alignment when we forfeit our soul. We need to take control of our soul in a healthy way.

## *Bringing the Soul Under Control*

So, how do we do that? Let's look at the definition of the word *spirit* for a moment. The definition for *spirit* mentions breath; it also mentions wind.[32] When we look at the various translations of the Hebrew and Greek words for wind, it is often used to refer to God's breath. Instead of being worried about our own breath in our soul, we can deeply inhale the breath of God.

Our spirit consists of our mind and our decisions. It governs the soul. Sometimes our soul stomps out our spirit because we're forfeiting our soul to the world. This is why Jesus said to Peter, "Get behind me, Satan!" (Matthew 16:23 ESV).

I triple-dog dare you to say, "Get behind me, Satan!" the next time you realize your soul is out of balance and taking over. Making a practice of that will help you to strengthen and build up your spirit. If we have a strong spirit, it will keep our soul under control and aligned with God's Spirit.

We need to ask God to identify the places in our lives where we are forfeiting our souls. As we work on those areas with God's help and guidance, we will bring our soul and our spirit into a beautiful and healthy balance. Like two evenly matched sumo wrestlers fighting in the ring, neither one overpowers the other.

Our spirit should be in constant communication with God's Spirit, who will help us to make wise decisions in alignment with His will and enable us to have strong moral character.

Second Timothy 1:7 tells us, "For God gave us a spirit not of fear but of power and love and self-control" (ESV). God's Spirit that He gives us is not weak or fearful. His Spirit consists of three main components: power, love, and self-control. Our spirit is not meant to be dominated by our soul. But sometimes, our spirit can get out of alignment because it's being dominated by one of those three components, instead of all three components being in balance.

You might be walking in a spirit of power and have an anointing to heal others, for example, but you have no love for them. It doesn't matter if your anointing is effective if you don't have love for the people you're healing (1 Corinthians 13:1–3).

Or maybe you do have love for the people you're healing, but you have no self-control. Maybe in your private life you have an addiction to pornography. Once again, your spirit is out of balance and is therefore not in alignment with God and His will.

We need to be mindful of the type of spirit God has given us. He has not given us a spirit of fear, so when we give into fear, we try coping in the ways that the world copes and we lose our self-control, our love, and our power. He did not give us fear, so don't give into it. Fear will weaken our spirit.

## *The Flesh Versus the Spirit*

Galatians 5:16–26 (ESV) offers further insight into the struggle for dominance between our soul and our spirit:

> *But I say, walk by the Spirit, and you will not gratify the desires of the flesh. For the desires of the flesh are against the Spirit, and the desires of the Spirit are against the flesh, for these are opposed to each other, to keep you from doing the things you want to do. But if you are led by the Spirit, you are not under the law. Now the works of the flesh are evident: sexual immorality, impurity, sensuality, idolatry, sorcery, enmity, strife, jealousy, fits of anger, rivalries, dissensions, divisions, envy, drunkenness, orgies, and things like these. I warn you, as I warned you before, that those who do such things will not inherit the kingdom of God. But the fruit of the Spirit is love, joy, peace, patience, kindness, goodness, faithfulness, gentleness, self-control; against such things there is no law. And those who belong to Christ Jesus have crucified the flesh with its passions and desires.*
>
> *If we live by the Spirit, let us also keep in step with the Spirit. Let us not become conceited, provoking one another, envying one another.*

Did you notice that what the Spirit wants is completely opposed to what the flesh wants (Galatians 5:17)? If we're spending all our time in our flesh, then the sumo wrestler that is our soul becomes a Yokozuna, which is the highest rank in sumo wrestling, and completely takes out the sumo wrestler that is our spirit. Our desires end up trumping the Spirit that God gave us.

We need to take these desires of the flesh, these desires that are not healthy, these desires that the soul sometimes tries to convince us are good for us when they're not, and we need to crucify them with Christ Jesus (Galatians 5:24).

We did this when we became Christians and accepted Jesus as our Lord and Savior, and it's something that we continue to do. We are already free from these works of the flesh because God nailed them to the cross with Jesus, but we need to keep reminding ourselves of that.

Jesus died for our transgressions, and His death set us free. God has given us the power of His Holy Spirit, and when we fully receive that Holy Spirit, the things of the flesh no longer take us out, because we know we live in complete freedom as a result of what Jesus did for us on the cross.

## *Benefits of the Holy Spirit*

The Holy Spirit does many things for us, but there are four in particular that I'd like to focus on. First, the Holy Spirit gives us power.

*1. We can walk in God's power because He gave us His Spirit.* Acts 1:8 states, "But you will receive power when the Holy Spirit comes on you; and you will be my witnesses in Jerusalem, and in all Judea and Samaria, and to the ends of the earth."

God gives us His power not so we can hold onto it ourselves but so we can be His witnesses and share His power with others, locally and globally. No matter where the Lord places you, He gives you His Spirit and His power so that you can be His witness. May we never be afraid to simply walk up to someone and ask if we can pray for them.

We are to walk in His power everywhere we go and recognize that it is a gift from God. We are to then exercise that gift so other people may receive it. Revival starts in your heart when you accept God's Holy Spirit and His power, and then it spreads to others like a wildfire.

*2. The Holy Spirit gives us God's love.* Romans 5:5 tells us, "And hope does not put us to shame, because God's love has been poured out into our hearts through the Holy Spirit, who has been given to us."

No matter what we are going through, we can live in tremendous hope because we have the love of the Father flowing through us.

*3. The Holy Spirit makes us more like Christ.* God wants us to reflect Jesus, His one and only begotten Son.

Second Corinthians 3:18 states, "So all of us who have had that veil removed can see and reflect the glory of the Lord. And the Lord—who is the Spirit—makes us more and more like him as we are changed into his glorious image" (NLT).

When we receive the Holy Spirit, we are better able to see God. We can see Him more easily in creation, in brokenness, and in other people because He has given us His Spirit of love and power. It's like having special Holy Spirit goggles that help us to see others the way God sees them and then reflect God to them.

*4. The Holy Spirit fills us with hope.* Romans 15:13 says, "May the God of hope fill you with all joy and peace as you trust in him, so that you may overflow with hope by the power of the Holy Spirit."

God has filled me with hope in the midst of my cancer diagnosis to the point where cancer doesn't scare me at all. And I pray the same for you. The world and the doctors and the hospital will try to fill you with fear with the things they say, but that fear has no place in your life.

## *Spiritual Wellness Is Worth It*

God wants us to have a balanced soul and a strong spirit so that our soul will not trample our spirit and take us out of alignment with His will and His ways. We are to set our hearts on the things of God, not the things of man, and on the desires of the Spirit, not the desires of the flesh.

This requires understanding the spirit that God has given us—a spirit of power, love, and self-control that causes us to overflow with hope. We do not have a spirit of fear but a spirit that enables us to see God, reflect Him to others, and grow in Christlikeness.

Making over our soul is a tough order, but with God's help, we can do it. Paul offers us this encouragement in Philippians 1:6, "And I am sure of this, that he who began a good work in you will bring it to completion at the day of Jesus Christ" (ESV).

A soul makeover sets us up for better health on this earth. And with our body, mind, and soul in an optimal state of wellbeing, we will be better prepared to handle whatever God may have for us in this life. We are better able to handle the attacks on our relationships and marriages from the enemy.

Remember the treasure God gave you, your spouse—he or she is absolutely worth fighting for. So suit up your sumo spirit, knowing God is your ultimate trainer!

# Chapter Seven Homework

**Question:** In what specific ways have you found yourself giving into the devil's schemes to scare you away from the purpose to which God has called you? What promises has God given you, directly or through His Word, to counter the devil's schemes?

_____

_____

_____

_____

_____

_____

_____

_____

_____

_____

**Question:** What is dominating your life—your soul or your spirit? Is your spirit in alignment with God and His will? Why or why not? If needed, what steps can you take to get back into alignment?

_____

_____

_____

_____

_____

_____

_____

_____

_____

_____

**Action:** Write down the list of the benefits of the Holy Spirit. For each benefit, write an example of how you see that benefit working in your life. Spend time asking God to reveal more of the benefits of the Holy Spirit in your life.

# *Chapter Seven Notes*

_____

_____

_____

_____

_____

_____

_____

_____

_____

_____

_____

_____

_____

_____

_____

_____

_____

_____

_____

_____

_____

_____

_____

CHAPTER EIGHT

# Hidden Treasure #8:
# Jesus Wants In Your Wagon

If you've read through the four Gospels, you've probably noticed that Jesus asked a lot of questions. God asked hundreds of questions throughout the other books of the Bible as well. Amazing questions. The kind of questions that make you stop and think for a moment before responding.

I've been asking a lot of questions myself these days due to my cancer diagnosis, so I've been taking a closer look at the questions Jesus asked in the Gospel of Mark. And as I'm reading and reflecting on those questions, God has been asking me other questions.

During a prophetic session with a group of fellow church leaders, I was asked these questions: "What is in your red wagon? What are your hopes and dreams and desires, and what do you want to see as you pull that red wagon along?"

Immediately, my heart was flooded with answers—some that were spiritual, and some that were more earthly and material. My brain was starting to spin, to be honest.[33]

But then, they asked me another one: "What if your wagon is empty? Is Jesus enough?"

That's a good question, isn't it? "Is Jesus enough?"

If you're pulling your red wagon down the road and there's nothing in it except Christ Himself, is that enough for you? Or do you want to squish Him into the back corner of the wagon and fill it up with all the things that you desire and that are on your heart?

### *Answering Jesus' Question with Faith*

The Gospel of Mark contains several questions that are helpful for us to consider as we reflect on what's in our red wagon.

In Mark 10:51, Jesus asked, "What do you want me to do for you?" This is one of those questions that just jumped out at me, and I couldn't let it go. Here's the context of Jesus' question:

> *Then they came to Jericho. As Jesus and his disciples, together with a large crowd, were leaving the city, a blind man, Bartimaeus (which means "son of Timaeus"), was sitting by the roadside begging. When he heard that it was*

*Jesus of Nazareth, he began to shout, "Jesus, Son of David, have mercy on me!"*

*Many rebuked him and told him to be quiet, but he shouted all the more, "Son of David, have mercy on me!"*

*Jesus stopped and said, "Call him."*

*So they called to the blind man, "Cheer up! On your feet! He's calling you." Throwing his cloak aside, he jumped to his feet and came to Jesus.*

*"What do you want me to do for you?" Jesus asked him.*

*The blind man said, "Rabbi, I want to see."*

*"Go," said Jesus, "your faith has healed you." Immediately he received his sight and followed Jesus along the road.*
**—Mark 10:46–52**

There was a blind man named Bartimaeus who was calling out to Jesus. He referred to Jesus as the Son of David, which basically meant that He was acknowledging Jesus as the Messiah. It would've been a risky move to say something like that out loud at the time, but when people told Bartimaeus to be quiet, he said it again even louder.

Prior to this, every time Jesus had performed a miracle in the Gospel of Mark, He had told the person He healed not to say anything about it. And then, of course, the person who was healed tells everybody anyways. But now that it was Palm Sunday and Jesus was about to enter Jerusalem, it was a different story. Jesus met Bartimaeus's request because of his faith, because of his heart, and because he was crying out loud to Him.

## *Answering Jesus' Question Incorrectly*

There's something interesting about the question Jesus asked Bartimaeus. It was the same question He asked of James and John, the sons of Zebedee, in Mark 10:36. Let's take a look at the context of that question:

> *Then James and John, the sons of Zebedee, came to him. "Teacher," they said, "we want you to do for us whatever we ask."*
>
> *"What do you want me to do for you?" he asked.*
>
> *They replied, "Let one of us sit at your right and the other at your left in your glory."*
>
> *"You don't know what you are asking," Jesus said. "Can you drink the cup I drink or be baptized with the baptism I am baptized with?"*
>
> *"We can," they answered.*
>
> *Jesus said to them, "You will drink the cup I drink and be baptized with the baptism I am baptized with, but to sit at my right or left is not for me to grant. These places belong to those for whom they have been prepared."*
>
> *When the ten heard about this, they became indignant with James and John. Jesus called them together and said, "You know that those who are regarded as rulers of the Gentiles lord it over them, and their high officials exercise authority over them. Not so with you. Instead, whoever wants to become great among you must be your servant, and whoever wants to be first must be slave of all. For even the Son of Man did not come to be served, but to serve, and to give his life as a ransom for many."*
>
> **—Mark 10:35–45**

Imagine that James and John were pulling their red wagons down the road, and they wanted to fill them with seniority and power and glory. They wanted Jesus to make them awesome. They still didn't quite understand who Jesus was, and they answered His question incorrectly.

Jesus then taught an amazing lesson to His followers. He made it clear to them that they were asking for the wrong thing, telling them, "If you want to be in glory, you need to become a servant. Watch what I'm about to do."

Jesus is the servant of all because of what He did for us on the cross. He gave His life as a ransom for us.

In this passage, Jesus used the question as a teaching moment because He knew their hearts were off. Their hearts were not in alignment with the kingdom of God and heaven coming here to earth.

Bartimaeus's heart, however, was in alignment because of his tremendous faith. He cried out to Jesus. And Jesus didn't just heal him on the spot; He asked the question, "What do you want me to do for you?"

I want you to understand the difference here. When we ask Jesus for something, we need to make sure our heart is in the right place. It's not about us and having our red wagon overflow with all the things we want. It's about our heart being in alignment with God's will. And when our heart is in alignment with God's will, Jesus might just be all that we need.

I have asked Jesus to heal my cancer, but if He does not, I have to ask myself, "Is Jesus still enough?"

## He Knows What Lies Ahead

*As they approached Jerusalem and came to Bethphage and Bethany at the Mount of Olives, Jesus sent two of his disciples, saying to them, "Go to the village ahead of you, and just as you enter it, you will find a colt tied there, which no one has ever ridden. Untie it and bring it here. If anyone asks you, 'Why are you doing this?' say, 'The Lord needs it and will send it back here shortly.'"*

*They went and found a colt outside in the street, tied at a doorway. As they untied it, some people standing there asked, "What are you doing, untying that colt?" They answered as Jesus had told them to, and the people let them go. When they brought the colt to Jesus and threw their cloaks over it, he sat on it. Many people spread their cloaks on the road, while others spread branches they had cut in the fields. Those who went ahead and those who followed shouted, "Hosanna!" "Blessed is he who comes in the name of the Lord!" Blessed is the coming kingdom of our father David!" "Hosanna in the highest heaven!"*

*Jesus entered Jerusalem and went into the temple courts. He looked around at everything, but since it was already late, he went out to Bethany with the Twelve.*
*—Mark 11:1–11*

The first question in Mark 11 is found in verse 3: "If anyone asks you, 'Why are you doing this?' say, 'The Lord needs it and will send it back here shortly.'" Jesus saw this situation coming before His disciples did, and He made sure that they were prepared for it.

I love this question because it shows us the authority that Jesus has in our lives. We may not know what's ahead of us, but He does.

You might have your own red-wagon plans, but you need to be in alignment with God's will. Jesus already knows your plans. And if He is enough, and He's along for the ride in your wagon, He already knows the plans He has for you.

Take the time to be prayerful in this season of your life and ask God what He has in store for you, for your family. Put yourself in a position of prayer and make Jesus enough.

## *Clearing Out Clutter in Your Wagon*

After the two disciples who were sent to get the colt had that amazing experience of Jesus' authority and fore-knowledge, they were greeted by an even more incredible sight. As Jesus entered Jerusalem, the crowd was spreading their cloaks and tree branches on the road, and they were shouting, "Hosanna," which means "Save!"[34] (Mark 11:8–10).

The people were already proclaiming that Jesus was their Savior, but their understanding of what that meant was a little skewed. They were thinking of Jesus as a king who would conquer the Roman Empire and restore their land and autonomy.

But that was not the King who had just entered Jerusalem. He rode in on a colt in gentleness and humility, not on a warhorse with full armor.

The people's words were definitely correct, but their minds were not necessarily aligned with God's kingdom, which we will see in the next part of Mark 11:

> *The next day as they were leaving Bethany, Jesus was hungry. Seeing in the distance a fig tree in leaf, he went to find out if it had any fruit. When he reached it, he found nothing but leaves, because it was not the season for figs. Then he said to the tree, "May no one ever eat fruit from you again." And his disciples heard him say it.*
>
> *On reaching Jerusalem, Jesus entered the temple courts and began driving out those who were buying and selling there. He overturned the tables of the money changers and the benches of those selling doves, and would not allow anyone to carry merchandise through the temple courts. And as he taught them, he said, "Is it not written: 'My house will be called a house of prayer for all nations'? But you have made it 'a den of robbers.'"*
>
> **—Mark 11:12–17**

Jesus was obviously frustrated regarding the state of the temple. I mean, He was flipping over tables and yelling at people that they should not be using worship in that way.

It makes me wonder if we do something similar. The Holy Spirit dwells inside of us, which makes us God's temple (1 Corinthians 3:16). Have we allowed God's temple to become a den of robbers? Where are our minds, our hearts, our souls? Do we need Jesus to come into us and clear us out?

Is the temple inside of you conducive to the Holy Spirit moving through you freely? If you're more concerned about what's in your wagon than you are about God's presence, you may want to ask God for His help with that. Instead of a den of robbers, we want our souls to be a place of worship and prayer.

## *Bearing Fruit*

*The chief priests and the teachers of the law heard this and began looking for a way to kill him, for they feared him, because the whole crowd was amazed at his teaching.*

*When evening came, Jesus and his disciples went out of the city.*

*In the morning, as they went along, they saw the fig tree withered from the roots. Peter remembered and said to Jesus, "Rabbi, look! The fig tree you cursed has withered!"*
**—Mark 11:18–21**

Remember how Jesus approached the fig tree to find some fruit to eat and saw nothing but leaves? There was no fruit. And then, He entered the temple, a place of worship, and saw nothing but money being exchanged. There was no fruit there, either.

He saw people who were only concerned about filling up their red wagons until they overflowed with merchandise and money instead of emptying their wagons and allowing God to fill them with what He desired.

God is calling us to not just bear leaves but to bear fruit, too. When He returns, I pray that He finds figs, not just leaves, on all of us.

This starts with God working in our innermost being. When we allow Him to work, it's amazing what He can do. As we start producing fruit, we will be able to encourage others to produce fruit as well. This is what the Lord is calling us to do.

## *Check for Gum Under Your Wagon*

Jesus responded to Peter's exclamation over the with-ered fig tree in Mark 11:22–25:

> *"Have faith in God," Jesus answered. "Truly I tell you, if an-yone says to this mountain, 'Go, throw yourself into the sea,' and does not doubt in their heart but believes that what they say will happen, it will be done for them. There-fore I tell you, whatever you ask for in prayer, believe that you have received it, and it will be yours. And when you stand praying, if you hold anything against anyone, forgive them, so that your Father in heaven may forgive you your sins."*

Peter didn't technically ask a question, but Jesus still provided an answer. It was a great lesson for His followers then, and it's a great lesson for us now. Here are two im-portant takeaways from that lesson.

1. The first is pretty straightforward: *belief.* Have faith in God, just like blind Bartimaeus did. And just as Bartimaeus asked for his sight, we should have the courage and the faith to ask God for anything.

2. If you're holding anything against anyone, you might want to clear out your inner temple. You might want to flip over your wagon and check underneath for gum. Take that gum and hand it over to Christ. It's not yours to continue to chew on, because it's taking you out. It's under

your red wagon, but it shouldn't be there. Clean it off.

*Forgiveness* is huge. A friend of mine on social media—a friend I held a lot of anger toward in the past—recently had a birthday. When the notification popped up letting me know it was their birthday, I had to check my heart. I had to flip over my wagon and check under it for gum.

The wagon was gum-free, and I praised God for helping me get to a place where I was able to completely forgive this person for something that happened to me years ago, which I had held onto for a long time.

I pray God would continue to remind me of any person I harbor resentment toward and help me to flip that wagon and see the gum, because I might be missing it. And I pray that for you as well, that you would be able to forgive before you approach God in prayer.

## *What We Can Do for God*

This brings us back to the question Jesus asked in Mark 10:51: "What do you want me to do for you?" It's a question Jesus is asking you and me today. And it's a question you and I should be asking Him, too. "Jesus, what do You want me to do for You?"

He recently answered that question for me. I thought He was going to give me a task, like pursuing a particular ministry. But do you know what He said? "Rest in Me. I am enough."

What would happen if you climbed into your red wagon and let God pull it? It's actually easier than you think. We need to get to a place where we allow Jesus to ask us, "Am I enough?" and then allow Him to help us.

How great is it that He asks the same question twice, in Mark 10:36 and Mark 10:51? And how amazing it is that we have a God who asks us that question at all: "What do you want me to do for you?"

When I asked Him that same question, I didn't expect Him to answer the way He did. But that's how God rolls. "Rest in Me. I am enough."

We have enough. Whether we're in the midst of difficulty or life is going smoothly, we have this living water, this bread of life, this blood that was sacrificed for us and washes away our sins. We need to remember how good our God is and find rest in our wagon.

# Chapter Eight Homework

**Question:** Is your heart in alignment with God? If your red wagon is empty, is Jesus enough? If God doesn't heal you, is Jesus enough?

_____

_____

_____

_____

_____

_____

_____

_____

_____

_____

_____

**Question:** Where are your mind, your heart, and your soul? Do you need Jesus to clear you out? Is the temple inside of you conducive to the Holy Spirit moving through you freely? Ask God for His help to enable you to be you're more concerned about God's presence than about what's in your wagon.

_____

_____

_____

_____

_____

_____

_____

_____

_____

_____

_____

**Action:** Spend some time in God's presence and ask, "Jesus, what do You want me to do for You?" In a notebook or journal, write down His response to you.

# *Chapter Eight Notes*

_____

_____

_____

_____

_____

_____

_____

_____

_____

_____

_____

_____

_____

_____

_____

_____

_____

_____

_____

_____

_____

CHAPTER NINE

# Hidden Treasure #9:
# Thankfulness in Action

My most recent PET scan showed that my cancer is getting worse. When we received the results, my first thought was, "I hope I live long enough to see my daughter and my son in their performances of *Annie the Musical* and *Willy Wonka Jr.*" Cayden played Annie's dog (it was super-cute), and Sierra played Mrs. Gloop in *Willie Wonka Jr.*

Both my kids love the stage. As a pastor who spends a lot of time on a stage, I'm guessing they got that trait from their daddy. The performances were both within weeks of each other, on two separate weekends. Each morning of the performance, I woke up and I thanked God. I woke up that Friday morning and I thanked God. I woke up that Saturday morning and I thanked God. I repeated the same pattern during the next weekend's performances.

I thanked Him when I woke up this morning, because God has blessed me along this journey. I am now almost five years into this cancer diagnosis, and every step of the way, God has been giving me these little hopes and promises.

I recently received prayer for healing at another church, and the woman who prayed over me told me, "Dan, you are not going to miss a thing." That struck me hard.

See, I'm not afraid of dying. I'm excited to go to heaven and be with Jesus—it's going to be awesome. But I do have two young children, and I want to watch them grow up. I want to be there for school plays and basketball games and graduations and weddings.

And I say this because the Lord has made these promises to me along the way. I continue to press forward on these prophetic promises that have been spoken over me.

When I was first diagnosed, a trusted friend told me they had a dream that I was going to be just fine. I have these words in my head that I hold onto because of the promises and the power of the Word of God.

As Shakespeare's character Henry VI said, "O Lord, that lends me life, lend me a heart replete with thankfulness!"[35] I am so very, very thankful to the Lord.

## *A Divine Dinner Reservation*

Another blessing for which I am tremendously grateful came in the form of a gift card given to me by a member of my congregation. It was for a gourmet dinner and an expensive bottle of wine at a posh hotel—a perfect getaway evening for Annette and me.

At the time, we were debating three different treatment options for this cancer, and none of the options was good. As we sipped our wine, we discussed and pondered and prayed over which of these options we should potentially choose.

During the conversation, I complimented my wife on her ability to encourage other people, whether she knows them or not. I told her how much I appreciate her amazing gift of encouragement.

There was another couple sitting a short distance from us, and the man turned to us and said, "Hey, I just want to let you know what a lovely couple you are."

I thanked him and said, "It's so interesting that you say that, as I was just complimenting my wife on her gift of encouragement, and here you are, encouraging us!"

His girlfriend asked if we knew who he was. We didn't. "Well," she said, "he's a pretty amazing guy, and one of the things that makes him so amazing is that he's a world-renowned cancer expert."

Here we were, having this discussion about these three treatment options that we didn't even like, and we were sitting within earshot of a cancer expert.

"Do you mind if we ask your opinion?" He didn't mind at all, and when we shared the three options with him, he immediately told us not to go with the second option. That was the treatment I had kind of been leaning toward, and he was able to step in and tell us not to go that direction.

This is the way the Lord works. He is guiding and directing every single step that we take. And this is cause for great thankfulness and praise.

## *Thankful for Grace*

Gratitude for the saints to whom he is writing is a theme in the opening of several of Paul's letters to the churches. We see one example of this in 1 Corinthians 1:4: "I always thank my God for you because of his grace given you in Christ Jesus."

This verse makes me think about the grace given to each and every one of us—this tremendous, amazing grace that God is giving to us as a gift every single moment of every single day. I encourage you to open your eyes and your ears to this amazing gift of grace today.

Paul further defined this God-given grace as a gift from the Holy Spirit that unites us to Jesus Christ. He encouraged us to hold onto this gift until Jesus returns:

> *For in him you have been enriched in every way—with all kinds of speech and with all knowledge—God thus confirming our testimony about Christ among you. Therefore you do not lack any spiritual gift as you eagerly wait for our Lord Jesus Christ to be revealed.*
> **—1 Corinthians 1:5–7**

Paul was thanking the church in Corinth and reminding them that they had been blessed by the gifts the Holy Spirit freely gives out. He described these gifts in greater detail in 1 Corinthians 12:7–11:

> *Now to each one the manifestation of the Spirit is given for the common good. To one there is given through the Spirit a message of wisdom, to another a message of knowledge by means of the same Spirit, to another faith by the same*

*Spirit, to another gifts of healing by that one Spirit, to another miraculous powers, to another prophecy, to another distinguishing between spirits, to another speaking in different kinds of tongues, and to still another the interpretation of tongues. All these are the work of one and the same Spirit, and he distributes them to each one, just as he determines.*

Wisdom, knowledge, faith, healing, miraculous powers, prophecy, discernment, speaking in tongues, interpretation of tongues—if you have all of those gifts of the Holy Spirit, or even if you have just one of those gifts, come hang out with me. We'll do lunch.

We need to come up with ways that we can leverage the gifts of the Spirit to become givers of thanks. Our goal is to go and distribute thanksgiving. We can be thankful for these gifts and lean into them, and we can identify and encourage them in other people. Build up the gift within yourself, and then leverage it for God's purposes to advance the kingdom of heaven here on earth.

## *Practicing Gratitude*

The last example of Paul's gratitude for the saints that we'll be focusing on is found in Romans 1:8: "First, I thank my God through Jesus Christ for all of you, because your faith is being reported all over the world."

What would it look like if we gave thanks in such a way that our faith in Christ was reported all over the world? Imagine if we had such grateful hearts that people took notice of the faith we have in Jesus.

God is calling our hearts to be in a posture of thankfulness even in the middle of the storm. We are called to be thankful saints in Christ Jesus.

Let's take our thankfulness and put it into action. Here are some simple, practical ways to do this.

- Give a thank-you note to someone who isn't expecting it.

- Send a bouquet of flowers to someone you appreciate.

- Say thank-you to kids for their help and their service to the Lord.

- Light a candle and focus on a recent blessing God has given you.

- Bring to dinner to someone who nurtures and cares for others.

- Make collages of the people, the places, and the opportunities for which you are most grateful. Laminate them and turn them into placemats. When people come over to your house and comment on the placemats, you'll be able to share about your thankfulness.

- Visit the websites of merchants who make or sell things you love and leave a positive review.

- Remember bad times—your frustrations, your failures, your losses—and consider how things have improved. Give thanks for your resilience and your

renewal, and then use that as a testimony for someone who's going through it.

- Speak up publicly at work, at church, and in your
  neighborhood, to highlight others' help and support. Your recognition might be exactly what that
  person needs to hear.

- Appreciate your pet by spending time with them.
  Pet them or play with them.

- Give attention and appreciation to people you
  know at the same level you give it to your pet.

## *Grateful for God's Love*

Once we learn the type of love that Jesus gave to us,
and can fully understand and embrace it, we will never
want to leave His side.

Can I tell you a little secret? Jesus never leaves your
side, ever. He's got you covered. He's above you, below
you, behind you, in front of you, to your right, to your left,
and surrounding you all of the time.

If we can just receive that love from our loving Father,
we will be able to give thanks to Him and give thanks to
others. Being surrounded by His love gives us a grateful
heart, even in the midst of the storm.

WORKBOOK

# Chapter Nine Homework

**Question:** Describe the ways you have witnessed God guiding and directing every single step you've taken in your experience with chronic illness. When you look at all the ways God has led you up to this point, what is your response? How does that impact your perspective moving forward?

_____

_____

_____

_____

_____

_____

_____

_____

_____

**Question:** How is God using you to distribute the thankfulness He has for us, through the gifts He has given you? Look at the list of simple, practical ways to put thankfulness into action. Choose one or a few of those things to do in the coming days and weeks.

_____

_____

_____

_____

_____

_____

_____

_____

_____

_____

**Action:** In a notebook or journal, write out all the words God has given you directly, through others, and through His Word that fill you with hope and joy. Read over this list and remind yourself of God's goodness whenever you begin to sense waves of discouragement.

## *Chapter Nine Notes*

_____

_____

_____

_____

_____

_____

_____

_____

_____

_____

_____

_____

_____

_____

_____

_____

_____

_____

_____

_____

_____

_____

CHAPTER TEN

# Hidden Treasure #10:
# Find Hope

When I was diagnosed with stage IV terminal cancer in 2017, the doctors told me I would have two years to live if I treated my cancer, or three to six months if I didn't treat it. At the time I am writing this, I have surpassed those expectations, being five years into my diagnosis.

Praise God that the doctors were wrong. I give Him all the glory for the journey thus far.

The only reason I can say this is because God is working on me, and one of the ways He's doing this is through the book of Romans. The promises of God that I have found in Romans have changed my heart and my mind forever, and I hope they will do the same for you.

## *My Path Thus Far*

First, let me give you a look back at my cancer journey with Jesus.

After my diagnosis in 2017, Annette and I changed our diets and embraced superfoods that might help combat the cancer. If you opened up our refrigerator early on in the process, you'd think it looked like a farmers' market. You'd see fresh fruits and vegetables in all the colors of the rainbow. We juiced, we blended, and we ate raw. We also did a lot of research and absorbed copious amounts of information on how to live a clean, healthy life.

I then started having blood tests done every quarter. The results revealed that the circulating tumor cells in my body were retracting, which we credited to this health and wellness track we were on.

Every time I went in for a PET scan, however, it showed that the cancer itself was actually growing. It was spreading up and down my spine and through my ribs at a fairly rapid rate. I had a PET scan every three to six months, and every time I went in, the results were discouraging. But my bloodwork was showing that the cancer was going away. It was a very confusing thing.

Meanwhile, the doctors had no idea where the cancer had started. My diagnosis was non-primary metastatic stage IV cancer, which meant that they could not determine the source of the cancer—whether it had started in my prostrate, brain, lungs, bones, etc. After a few DNA tests, however, they determined that it was most likely prostate cancer, with a slight chance of it being breast cancer.

I continued to do all sorts of tests, including the bloodwork and the PET scans. We sought a second opinion from another hospital, and they suggested that I have another type of DNA test.

Prior to that, my oncologists had said that there was a ninety-percent chance it was prostate cancer, and they had prescribed a significant treatment plan. The traditional protocol they were recommending was lonely, painful, and poisonous. It's brutal stuff, as anyone who has been through that protocol, or knows someone who has, is aware.

The results of the DNA test recommended by the other hospital, however, said that there was a ninety-percent chance it was breast cancer. Breast cancer has a completely different treatment protocol than prostate cancer. Both involve chemotherapy, but prostate cancer is associated with testosterone and breast cancer is associated with estrogen, which may impact the course of treatment.

Annette and I were even more confused. We had no idea what to do.

## *A Second Second Opinion*

At this point, it was June 2019. The pain in my body was getting increasingly worse on a daily basis. After five or six months of chronic pain, I went for a walk with Annette, in January 2020.

I told her, "Based on how my body's feeling and how the pain is escalating, I don't think I have much time left." It was a sad conversation to have with my bride.

Right after that, I received a phone call from a social worker at one of the hospitals. She asked if I had heard about a non-profit organization called the*second*opinion. Adult cancer patients in California can send them their medical records, and the organization will assemble a team of retired or semi-retired doctors to take a look at them for free.

Since I had two conflicting DNA test results, with one saying there was a ninety-percent chance it was prostate cancer and the other saying there was a ninety-percent chance it was breast cancer, I figured this was a great opportunity to get a bunch of eyeballs on my medical records.

A few weeks after we sent them the necessary information, Annette and I found ourselves sitting in front of a team of elderly, retired medical professionals. I felt like I was sitting in a room full of grandparents who really cared about me. They asked me really good questions about my whole plant-based diet, what I was doing and why I was doing it. They also asked about my soy protein intake, which I appreciated because of the conflicting research regarding soy and its potential connection to breast cancer. Soy may increase breast cancer risk, so if it turned out to be breast cancer, I would have to find out if soy intake might influence my risk.[36]

Their consensus was that the cancer I have is breast cancer, and they asked if I would be interested in the least toxic treatment option. Of course, I was.

So I started a new treatment plan at the end of February 2020, in which I would take one low-dose chemotherapy pill and an estrogen blocker. I would take the two pills every day for twenty-one days, take a week off, and then repeat the cycle. And keep repeating it.

I celebrated my fiftieth birthday on March 16 of that year in Lake Tahoe with my family. For fun, my daughter, Sierra, and I decided to film ourselves doing a Bollywood dance routine. After doing this four-minute dance routine with my daughter, it hit me that I didn't have any pain.

I was pain-free. Hallelujah!

Although that experience was short-lived, God is good, and we had been prayerfully paying attention to the path He had us on. I have been surrounded by a cloud of witnesses who are praying over me and my life, and I really feel like God has been directing our steps.

Am I out of the woods yet? Nope. My PET scans still indicate that I have stage IV cancer. My cancer is still metastatic, my pain levels are increasing, and I have side effects from morphine to control pain. But God is *with* me.

## *Christian Hope Perseveres and Endures*

I shouldn't be alive at this point, but here I am. So, what's the reason? Why am I here?

Maybe it's to offer you a message of hope. Let's talk about that.

There's a difference between hope and Christian hope. According to Romans, Christian hope is characterized by two elements: perseverance and endurance. These qualities make hope unique if you follow Jesus.

Christian hope also requires us to wait. Perseverance, endurance, and waiting are usually not part of my vocabulary. I'm impatient. I need stuff now.

But as I have walked through cancer with Jesus, I've learned important lessons on these subjects—lessons that are backed up by Scripture. Romans 5:1–4 (NET) has this to say about Christian hope:

> *Therefore, since we have been declared righteous by faith, we have peace with God through our Lord Jesus Christ, through whom we have also obtained access into this grace in which we stand, and we rejoice in the hope of God's glory. Not only this, but we also rejoice in sufferings, knowing that suffering produces endurance, and endurance, character, and character, hope.*

First of all, we need to have faith in the Lord (Romans 5:1). He then declares us righteous, which means that all of our sins, all of our mistakes, have been wiped clean. We have been set free from all of that. We are given freedom when we follow the Lord.

To put it mildly, my past isn't the greatest. Let's just say I wasn't always a pastor and leave it at that. But because of Christ, I am no longer chained to my past. Jesus has set me free.

I can stand confidently because of my faith in God's grace, in God's forgiveness, and in God's mercy (Romans 5:2). His grace, forgiveness, and mercy are also the only reasons that I'm still here. I can be reminded of this truth each and every day and embrace it with gratitude.

We worship and praise the Lord, and rejoice in Him, because we know that someday, we will be in His glory (Romans 5:2). Scripture reminds us that we are foreigners and exiles in this world (1 Peter 2:11–12). We're just here for a quick little visit before we move into eternal life. When we say yes to the Lord, we have eternal life in His glory.

We also rejoice in our sufferings (Romans 5:3). Most of us are suffering with something in our lives. And if you aren't suffering right now, chances are you know someone who is. Can you imagine if we actually started rejoicing in that?

That concept might just be a game-changer for you. We rejoice in our suffering not because of the suffering itself but because of the fruit it produces—endurance, character, and hope (Romans 5:3–4).

I have cancer. Can I rejoice in that? That sounds crazy. I'm not supposed to rejoice. I've had Christian brothers and sisters tell me not to rejoice, and not even to bring up the word "cancer."

But that's not what the Word of God says. And I am going to do what the Word says, regardless of what others may think.

I am going to rejoice in my cancer because I know it's creating this beautiful perseverance and endurance in me that's building my character day by day. If the Lord gives me tomorrow, I hope that I'm a better person tomorrow than I am today. And I hope my character has developed in such a way that it produces more hope inside of me.

Romans 5:5 then tells us what hope accomplishes: "And hope does not put us to shame, because God's love has been poured out into our hearts through the Holy Spirit, who has been given to us."

When we say yes to the Lord, the Holy Spirit is given to us as a free gift. And when we have this Christian hope, there is nothing for us to be ashamed about. We don't have to be ashamed of what we did in our past, what we did today, or what might happen tomorrow, because we have this hope through the Holy Spirit, who has been given freely to us.

God wants you to have the Holy Spirit. All you have to do is say yes and accept Him.

## *Christian Hope Involves Waiting*

Christian hope is characterized by perseverance and endurance, and Christian hope also requires us to wait. Romans 8:24–25 tells us, "For in hope we were saved. Now hope that is seen is not hope, because who hopes for what he sees? But if we hope for what we do not see, we eagerly wait for it with endurance" (NET).

If you already have what you've been hoping for, then there's no need to hope. I hope that someday I will be cancer-free. If I were cancer-free today, I wouldn't have to hope for it, because I'd already be cancer-free.

I hope that I can look back on the hope I've expressed to be healed of my cancer and praise God because He has fulfilled that hope. In the meantime, my character is building up because I'm persevering through the suffering, and that allows me to hope.

Not only does Scripture call us to rejoice in our suffering, but we are also to wait eagerly and with endurance for the things we are hoping for. It's like a kid the night before Christmas, sitting there with eagerness and hope of what's to come as they wait for Santa to bring them presents.

Whatever it is that you're hoping for, congratulations—it's Christmas Eve for you. You can wait with eagerness, saying, "Yes, Lord. I'm so excited to see my hope fulfilled!"

Christian hope requires us to be still and to know that He is God (Psalm 46:10). It also requires us to know that He is God and we are not. Sometimes we need to let God be God and acknowledge that we are pieces of clay He is shaping for His purposes, smoothing out our rough edges. We need to let Him shape us the way He wants to shape us. That process of shaping and waiting builds my character and makes me a better man, a better husband, a better father, a better pastor, a better professor.

Romans 12:12 reminds us, "Rejoice in hope, be patient in tribulation, be constant in prayer" (ESV). I encourage you to be constant in prayer. It's not as hard as you might think it is. It's simply having a conversation with your heavenly Father, who loves you more than any father you've ever had.

You can talk to Him about anything—even about how you're feeling toward Him. Are you angry at God? Tell Him. He's a big God. He can handle it.

You can thank Him for giving you the patience to endure the suffering you're experiencing right now. And you can ask Him to give you that endurance tomorrow as well.

If you have these conversations with God constantly, you'll be amazed by the results. God will take away your fear, your anxiety, and the burdens that you're carrying.

First Peter 5:7 encourages us, "Cast all your anxiety on him because he cares for you," and that's exactly what we're doing. We're handing everything over to the Lord through constant conversation with Him.

## *Trust in Him*

I love this prayer that Paul prayed over the Roman believers in Romans 15:13: "May the God of hope fill you with all joy and peace as you trust in him, so that you may overflow with hope by the power of the Holy Spirit."

We have a God of hope. How great is it, that we don't have a God of shame, or a God of putting us down, or a God of beating us up?

We need to trust our God of hope with everything that we're going through. I don't understand why one of my DNA tests indicated a ninety-percent chance of prostate cancer and the other indicated a ninety-percent chance of breast cancer, but I just need to hand that over to Him.

God is the problem-solver. He knows the details of my life. He knows the path that He has for me, and He knows the path that He has for you. And He is worthy of our trust.

My prayer is that you would develop a deeper level of trust in the Lord, even in the midst of suffering. May you rejoice in Him and give Him your fear, your burdens, and your anxiety. He has guided my every step on this cancer journey, and I know He will guide your journey as well.

This isn't about me and my story. It's about God and His story, and the ways in which He weaves His story into each and every one of us. I am so grateful and so full of hope.

None of us knows when our final day on earth will be. I don't know if I'll be here tomorrow or not, but there is a deep-rooted message of hope building up inside of me. And that is regardless of my final day.

# Chapter Ten Homework

**Question:** Is your life characterized by the elements of Christian hope: perseverance and endurance? If not, why? What can you do to embrace Christian hope?

_____

_____

_____

_____

_____

_____

_____

_____

_____

_____

_____

_____

**Question:** What is your response when you hear the phrase, "Rejoice in your suffering"? What kind of perspective shift would it require for you to be able to rejoice in your suffering? What has God made available for you to be able to do that?

_____

_____

_____

_____

_____

_____

_____

_____

_____

_____

_____

**Action:** In a notebook or journal, write a prayer of trust to God.

## *Chapter Ten Notes*

AFTERWORD

# Love, Me

The three letters that follow are expressions of love and encouragement for my wonderful kids and my beloved wife. My heart will always be with them, whether I'm here on earth or at home with the Lord.

*My goal is that they will be encouraged and knit together by strong ties of love.* I want them to have full confidence because they have complete understanding of God's secret plan, which is Christ Himself. In Him lie hidden all the treasures of wisdom and knowledge (Colossians 2:2–3).

Dear Cayden (a.k.a. Thunder),

I wanted to let you know how proud I am of you. I love watching you grow into a young man. I love the person you are, and I love the person you are becoming.

When Mom was pregnant with you and we found out that we were having a boy, I was so thrilled that my bloodline would be extended through a son as well as a daughter.

I remember reading through the Bible one night during the pregnancy and coming across Mark 3, where Jesus appoints His twelve disciples. Jesus gave the name *Boanerges* to James and his brother John, which means "sons of thunder."

I thought to myself, "How cool is it that Jesus referred to two of His closest followers as 'sons of thunder'?" I immediately began referring to you as Thunder. Mom was only three months pregnant with you.

When people asked me what we were going to name you, I would say, "We're going to name him Thunder." They didn't take me seriously, but God did.

The day you were born—August 6, 2009—there was a thunderstorm right above the hospital. I knew it was a prophetic sign on your life that you were going to bring the thunder.

So, what does it mean to bring the thunder? You see, like James and John, you were born to be a game-changer. Jesus knew this about His followers, and I know this about you.

James and John were far from perfect. They made mistakes as they followed and learned from Jesus. Trust me, I have made many mistakes as I have followed and learned from Jesus.

My biggest hurdle has been learning not to be so prideful. When you read about James and John in the Bible, you will see that they also struggled with pride. Being prideful means having an excessively high opinion of oneself.

If I have one lesson to teach you, it would be to never think of yourself as being better than anyone else. When we do, our heavenly Father has a way of pruning us into a posture of humility.

When James and John asked Jesus if they could sit at His right and His left in glory, Jesus replied, "Whoever wants to become great among you must be your servant, and whoever wants to be first must be slave of all" (Mark 10:43–44).

It is a simple lesson, Cayden: if you want to be great, you serve others. By serving others, you will be Thunder here on earth as it is in heaven.

I have already witnessed your amazing ability to do this well. I love watching you when you join me in serving the homeless community, or when we visit older adults in our church, or when you do something for someone else without even asking if they needed help in the first place.

You have a heart for the smallest of insects and the

largest of dogs, and you have an amazing ability to put people at ease, to make them laugh and smile, to show them gratitude.

You were born with these qualities, and I know they will serve you well no matter what you decide to do in life. Apply these qualities and the gift of your emotional intelligence to your family, friends, and strangers. These qualities will breathe life into others, just as Jesus and His disciples did for the communities they blessed during His ministry.

Another thing I love about you is that you are never satisfied. I know I joke with you about this, but it could work to your benefit if you manage this trait well. It could also bite you in the butt if you don't.

You seem to be persistent until things work in your favor. This is a great way to accomplish your life goals. However, if you are persistent in pursuing things that are not good for your mind, your body, or your soul, you risk falling into self-made traps.

Rather than listing things you should not be persistent about, let me list some things you should be persistent about in your life. Persistently seek:

- Love
- Forgiveness
- Truth
- Integrity
- Peace
- Kindness
- Joy
- Purpose

Don't be satisfied until you are constantly giving and receiving the traits listed above.

You see, your actual birth name is Cayden. This was a name that Mom picked out. I really wanted to name you Thunder, but then I found out the meaning of Cayden: spirit of battle.

Wow! My son, Thunder, also carries the spirit of battle. God's Spirit is inside of you, Cayden, and He created you to stand powerfully in the gap for others as it relates to love, forgiveness, truth, integrity, peace, kindness, joy, and purpose.

So, the next time you come across someone who is lacking one or more of those traits, bring on the thunder!

With all my love,
Dad (of Thunder)

Dear Sierra,

Before you were born, your mom and I had difficulty getting pregnant. This was then followed by the loss of two babies through miscarriage. As you might imagine, these were sad times for us. However, even though we were sad, we carried hope because of the simple fact  that we knew Mom could get pregnant.

And then, we got pregnant again with you. I knew in my spirit that you were going to stick around.

I have two distinct memories from our doctors' appointments during the pregnancy. The first memory is from our very first visit to the doctor. They placed an ultrasound device on Mom's belly, and it showed a bright, flashing light.

That light was your heartbeat. I remember thinking, "Of course God would use light to represent life." Jesus Himself said, "I am the light of the world. Whoever follows me will never walk in darkness, but will have the light of life" (John 8:12). It was confirmation yet again in my spirit that you were special and highly favored by the Lord.

The second memory is from another ultrasound. I distinctly remember how clearly I was able to see the profile of your face. I was seriously blown away by your beauty. I couldn't wait to meet you, but it was as if I already knew you.

I can't explain it, but you and I have an amazing bond. I'm sure many dads think they have an amazing bond with their daughter, but it is a fact that ours is different.

I can often tell that you know what I'm thinking and how I'm feeling without me having to say a word. Sometimes it creeps me out, but I am mostly in awe of how God has put us together in this lifetime.

I'm not sure if you know this, but every single day of Mom's pregnancy with you, I would bless your spirit, out loud, right into Mom's belly. If you don't believe me, you can ask her.

I would say something like, "Sierra, I call your spirit to attention. I bless you with abundant peace, wisdom, knowledge, and strength in the name of Jesus." I did this every day for two reasons: I wanted you to recognize my voice, and I wanted you to know and experience the power behind the name of Jesus.

The day you were born—October 30, 2007—you came out of Mom in a complete state of peace despite the thirty-six-hour labor. The doctor and the nurses even commented on how calm you were. I remember saying, "Hi, Sierra," and your eyes fixed on me as if you recognized my voice.

Then, all of a sudden, *boom!* An earthquake shook the entire hospital. The doctor threw herself over you and Mom, as Mom held you. I, however, was at complete peace, and so were you.

You see, I knew in the moment that the earthquake was

a prophetic sign from the Lord that you have been set apart. That you are highly favored.

Fast-forward twelve months, as you were first learning to walk. I remember thinking how clumsy you were. You were constantly crashing into walls and smashing your face on tables.

What tripped me out was that you never cried. You would slam your face into the corner of a table, end up with a welt on your head, and never make a peep. You seemed at peace with it. Strange, huh? Mom and I would joke, "Well, I guess she isn't going to be an athlete."

Fast-forward to age four, when we put you on a recreational soccer team. I didn't think much about the potential outcome of your first game since it was a bunch of four- and five-year-olds playing a confusing sport for the first time.

However, when the whistle blew, you ran straight for the ball, dodged the other players, and zoomed down the field to score a goal while three other girls were trying to tackle you from behind.

You went on to score five goals in a matter of minutes, and I remember thinking, "Hmm, maybe we were wrong about her athletic ability."

Fast-forward to the fifth grade. I was watching you play on the elementary school basketball team, and you were completely dominating. You scored at will. It was ten to two in the first period, and you had scored all ten points.

But then I witnessed something amazing. You completely stopped shooting the ball. I remember wondering why you did that. On your own, without the coach saying a word, at nine years old, you decided that you wanted everyone on your team to make a basket.

I was so proud that you understood the concept of a team at such an early age. You instinctively knew that a team is more important than an individual.

Fast-forward to today, when you were the first twelve-year-old invited to be the setter on the travel volleyball team for fourteen-year-olds. The setter position is easily the most important position on the team because you will be calling the plays, communicating positions, and giving everyone else the opportunity to receive the glory.

It reminds me of when the angel Gabriel told Mary that she was highly favored and that she was going to be the mother of the Lord. Mary said, "Behold, I am the servant of the Lord; let it be to me according to your word" (Luke 1:38 ESV).

Mary could have said, "Look at me! I'm awesome! God picked me!" But she took the role of a servant and allowed God to work freely in her life. She had the right mindset at such a young age. So do you, Sierra.

Your name is the Spanish word for mountain range. I remember the day God whispered your name in my ear before you were born. I knew right away that it was the perfect name for you because it connotes strength and groundedness.

You are a gift. You carry tremendous spiritual, physical, mental, and emotional strength, groundedness, and joy (your middle name).

As I write this letter, I can hear you in your room practicing the ukulele. I have peeked at the worship songs you are beginning to write. I love the person you are and the person you are becoming. I marvel at your work ethic (that you obviously got from your mama), and I cannot wait to see what the Lord does with your life.

With all my love,
Dad (of Sierra Joy)

Dear Sillypants (a.k.a. Annette),

The other night while we were sitting at the table, you were sharing the highlights of your day. This happened to be the week we found out the cancer was spreading despite the new medication I was taking (back in September 2020).

As you might remember, you, the kids, and I were experiencing raw emotions. I remember looking at your swollen eyes as you tried to cheerfully share about the exciting things happening at work.

You looked at me and noticed that my eyes were welling up with tears. "So why are you now crying?" you asked.

"I just love you," I said. But that isn't why I was crying. The reason my eyes were welling up was because I heard God say to me, "She has been the greatest blessing I have given you in your fifty years. Don't cling tight. You need to let her go."

"How in the #&@$ am I going to let her go?" I was pissed.

"What have you done with the cancer?" God asked calmly.

"I handed the cancer over to You, to let You deal with it."

"Now you must do the same with Annette and let Me be God."

"Fine!" I replied, still pissed.

This interaction between God and me has happened at least a dozen times in the years since my diagnosis, leading up to that critical moment at the table. I was so angry that I couldn't help you process things emotionally and mentally.

The truth is that dealing with cancer sucks for the both of us for different reasons. But dealing with the impact cancer has had on our marriage was something I would never have predicted or wished for in a million years.

So, here's what happened in that moment: I let go. I handed my beautiful wife over to God.

God said, "Just breathe. I've got this. She is precious to Me. She is precious to you. She is a blessing to Me. She is a blessing to you. I can handle this, but you need to let go."

So, I let go.

In order of importance, my two biggest prayers are that God will heal our marriage and that God will heal my cancer. As I write this, I'm not sure if He is going to do either. And I am finally okay with this. Crazy, huh?

The reason I am now okay with this is because I've realized that God has blessed me with an amazing wife and He has blessed me with an amazing life. You see, you are easily the best thing that has ever happened to me. Period!

I have so much dang love for you. We have had so many incredible memories together. We have raised two of the best children this side of the equator. My life simply would not be as amazing as it is if I didn't have such an amazing wife.

The day we got married, I knew we were in for a wild ride. It started with the sharing of our wedding vows at St. Paul's Church in the middle of a cornfield in Arlington, Nebraska. As we shared our vows, my mom later told me, the most amazing light from the sun broke through the stained-glass windows of the church and surrounded us. As we held hands in front of God, our family, our friends, and a bunch of Nebraskans I had never met before, we made a covenant promise.

But when my mom told me about the vision she saw of the light of the sun surrounding us, I knew in the moment that it was a prophetic sign from the Son that He had us surrounded all of our days—no matter what.

Before we got on the hayrack ride from the church to the high school gymnasium for our reception, you and I had a moment alone on the playground swings in front of the church. I remember how much fun it was to be dressed up in a tuxedo as I pushed you from behind on the swing. Your wedding dress was puffing up and then dragging in the dirt, and neither of us cared. We were too caught up in the blissfulness of the moment.

The next day, your mom came up to me and remarked on the playground swing moment, which she and your dad had witnessed on their way to the reception. "You got to experience the joy of the Lord on your wedding day as you pushed our daughter in that swing," she said.

I knew in the moment that her words were a prophetic sign that our marriage was going to be filled with complete Joy of the Lord (Joy, your middle name).

My head is flooded with all the reasons why I love you.

A ton of them are sexual (sorry to start here). Prior to this cancer, our sex life was off-the-charts exciting, and I am so grateful that God matched me with the perfect hump-mate (lol)! I'm bummed that cancer has wreaked havoc on our physical connection, but my memories alone could win us an X-rated Oscar—and the book would be a best-seller.

I love your quirks. I am not going to publicly list them here because I know I already embarrassed you enough with that last paragraphs.

Okay, sorry, just one. You love your routines, and I love the fact that you love your routines. If one of your routines gets out of routine, you quickly adjust to a new routine because you love routines.

I love your routines. I love that about you. It makes me smile so wide my face just might snap.

I love watching you be a mom. You are so good with Cayden. He hammers you with meaning-of-life questions all the time, and you just let him flow. You respond to him with such wisdom and grace. He has my mini-me personality and mind. The fact that you can handle having two males in the house who have the attention span of a gold-fish and the memory of a chicken is %@#$ing incredible.

You are just as good with Sierra, even though you may not think so. Your personalities and abilities are exactly alike: introverts, joy seekers, sharp as knives, superstar athletes, multitaskers, multitalented, huge hearts, the best listeners, moral compasses, beautiful voices—I could go on.

I can see times when you both snap because you both are never wrong. Cayden and I are always wrong, by the way, but you two are never wrong.

I don't say that as a judgment on your characters. I honestly believe that both of you are never wrong. I often find that I blame the two of you for something stupid, only to later find out that it was my fault or Cayden's fault. The dichotomy in our household cracks me up.

I do want to encourage you to allow Sierra to be right more often (even if she's not). I believe that her trust in you will continue to blossom as she matures into a young woman.

I often see moms and daughters struggle in their relationship. I believe that if Sierra sees that her mom trusts her judgment and allows her to make mistakes on her own, she will grow in her respect for Mama Bear.

It's kind of like the coaching philosophy that you and I both admire. Coaches who guide and correct during practice but are quiet during games allow athletes to self-assess and make the necessary adjustments for themselves. Model well for Sierra how to lead a good life, and then let her settle into the self-assessment mindset.

Most importantly, Honeybutt, you have been and will continue to be my Proverbs 31 wife. You have unmatched noble character, and you are worth far more than rubies. I lack nothing in value because I have you; you bless me with your goodness.

You provide so much for our family on a daily basis, and you work your @$$ off to make sure we are all thriving. You are so strong physically (such a hot body, by the way), and you provide that strength for so many others inside and outside our family.

I have so much respect for you, and I sing your praises

everywhere I go. You speak with such great wisdom and encouragement. Your faith is so strong; our children love you and are blessed because of you.

As you know, I am part chick. Because of that, I have been raised by and led by, and I work in professions that surround me with, really great women. But one thing is for sure: you surpass them all. I will continue to praise you here on earth and in heaven.

Finally, Sillypants, I am not sure who the Lord is going to take home first, me or you. Statistically, it seems I drew the short straw. If I go home sooner rather than later, please know that I know that you and the kids will not only be fine, but will thrive.

God has spoken very clearly to me since I said yes to Jesus in 2001 (thanks to you). And in my clear communication with Him, He has assured me that He has you and the kids in the palm of His hand.

With all my heart,
Goofball, husband of Annette Joy McClure
(a.k.a. Sillypants)

REFERENCES

# Notes

1. Tomlin, Chris. "Amazing Grace (My Chains Are Gone)." Track 11 on *See the Morning*. Sparrow Records/Passion Conference, 2006.

2. AC/DC. "Back in Black." Track 6 on *Back in Black*. Albert Productions/Atlantic Recording Corporation, 1980.

3. AC/DC. "Thunderstruck." Track 1 on *The Razors Edge*. ATCO Records, 1990.

4. AC/DC. "T.N.T." Track 3 on *T.N.T.* Albert Productions, 1976.

5. Boberg, Carl Gustav. "How Great Thou Art." 1949. Hymnary.org. https://hymnary.org/text/o_lord_my_god_when_i_in_awesome_wonder.

6. American Cancer Society. "Cancer Treatment and Survivorship Facts and Figures 2019–2021." https://www.cancer.org/content/dam/cancer-org/research/cancer-facts-and-statistics/cancer-treatment-and-survivorship-facts-and-figures/cancer-treatment-and-survivorship-facts-and-figures-2019-2021.pdf.

7. American Cancer Society. "Lifetime Risk of Developing or Dying

from Cancer." January 13, 2020. https://www.cancer.org/cancer/cancer-basics/lifetime-probability-of-developing-or-dying-from-cancer.html.

8. AC/DC. "Shot in the Dark." Track 3 on *Power Up.* Columbia Records/Sony Music Entertainment Australia, 2020.

9. Stuart, Mel, dir. *Willy Wonka and the Chocolate Factory.* Paramount Pictures, 1971.

10. Mikkelson, David. "Thomas Edison on the 'Doctor of the Future.'" Snopes Media Group Inc. January 25, 2015. https://www.snopes.com/fact-check/the-doctor-of-the-future/.

11. CNBC. "Buger King Scrapping 'Have It Your Way' Slogan." May 19, 2014. https://www.cnbc.com/2014/05/19/burger-king-scrapping-have-it-your-way-slogan.html.

12. American Cancer Society. "Cancer Facts and Figures 2021." https://www.cancer.org/content/dam/cancer-org/research/cancer-facts-and-statistics/annual-cancer-facts-and-figures/2021/cancer-facts-and-figures-2021.pdf.

13. American Cancer Society. "Cancer Facts & Figures 2018." https://www.cancer.org/content/dam/cancer-org/research/cancer-facts-and-statistics/annual-cancer-facts-and-figures/2018/cancer-facts-and-figures-2018.pdf.

14. *Encyclopædia Britannica*, "World War I 1914–1918: Killed, Wounded, and Missing." https://www.britannica.com/event/World-War-I/Killed-wounded-and-missing.

15. *Encyclopædia Britannica,* "World War II 1939–1945: Costs of the War." https://www.britannica.com/event/World-War-II/Costs-of-the-war.

16. The U.S. National Archives and Records of Administration. "Vietnam War U.S. Military Fatal Casualty Statistics." https://www.archives.gov/research/military/vietnam-war/casualty-statistics.

17. *Encyclopædia Britannica,* "September 11 Attacks: United States 2001." https://www.britannica.com/event/September-11-attacks/The-September-11-commission-and-its-findings.

18. Griswold, S. *Created to Heal Strong.* CreateSpace Independent Publishing Platform, 2018.

19. Prostate Cancer Foundation. "The Science of Living Well, Beyond Cancer." 2019, p. 68–69. https://res.cloudinary.com/pcf/image/upload/v1575394191/WellnessGuide_interactive_rev12.2.19_yrdiph.pdf.

20. Palikuca, Seka. "The Anti-Inflammatory Diet: 5 Things to Know." American Osteopathic Association. May 8, 2019. https://thedo.osteopathic.org/2019/05/the-anti-inflammatory-diet-5-things-to-know/#:~:text=Foods%20that%20cause%20inflammation%20include,processed%20meat%2C%20and%20red%20meat.

21. Center for Disease Control and Prevention. "Health and Economic Costs of Chronic Diseases." https://www.cdc.gov/chronicdisease/about/costs/index.htm.

22. Mokdad, Ali H., Katherine Ballestros, Michelle Echko, Scott Glenn, Helen E. Olsen, Erin Mullany, Alex Lee, et al. "The State of US Health, 1990–2016: Burden of Diseases, Injuries, and Risk Factors Among US States." *JAMA* 319, no. 14 (April 10, 2018): p. 1444–1472. doi: 10.1001/jama.2018.0158.

23. Center for Disease Control and Prevention. "2018 State Indicator Report on Fruits and Vegetables." https://www.cdc.gov/nutrition/

downloads/fruits-vegetables/2018/2018-fruit-vegetable-report-508. pdf.

24. Produce for Better Health Foundation. "About the Buzz: Eat 10 Servings of Fruits and Vegetables Per Day?" https://fruitsandveggies. org/stories/buzz-eat-10-servings-fruits-vegetables-per-day/.

25. Ballerini, Kelsea. "Unapologetically." Track 10 on *Unapologetically.* Black River, 2017.

26. *Bible Hub,* "talent." https://biblehub.com/topical/t/talent.htm.

27. *Blue Letter Bible,* "Strong's G5–abba." https://www.blueletter bible.org/lang/lexicon/lexicon.cfm?Strongs=G5&t=CSB.

28. Engle, Karen. "What Does 'Abba' Really Mean?" Logos. March 2021. https://blog.logos.com/what-does-abba-really-mean/.

29. *Urban Dictionary,* "pity party." https://www.urban dictionary.com/define.php?term=pity%20party.

30. *Merriam-Webster,* "psychoneuroimmunology." https://www .merriam-webster.com/dictionary/psychoneuroimmunology.

31. Cancer Research Institute. "Cancer and the Immune System: The Vital Connection." 2017. https://www.cancerresearch.org/CRI/media /PDF-Content/Cancer-and-the-Immune-System_2017-final_print. pdf.

32. *Blue Letter Bible,* "Strong's H7307–rûaḥ." https://www.blueletter bible.org/lang/lexicon/lexicon.cfm?strongs=H7307.

33. Sandoz, Gary. *Super Vintage Wagon.* November 19, 2017. Digital photograph. Unsplash. https://unsplash.com/photos/woi5ThOdQb4.

34. *Blue Letter Bible,* "Strong's G5614–hosanna." https://www.blue letterbible.org/lang/lexicon/lexicon.cfm?Strongs=G5614&t=KJV.

35. Shakespeare, William. *Henry VI: Part II,* 1.1.23–24. 1623. John Cawthorn, 1813, p. 6.

36. Zeratsky, Katherine. "Will Eating Soy Increase My Risk of Breast Cancer?" Mayo Clinic. https://www.mayoclinic.org/healthy-lifestyle /nutrition-and-healthy-eating/expert-answers/soy-breast-cancer-risk/ faq-20120377.

# About the Author

Dan McClure, M.A. is recognized as an expert in fitness, aging, nutrition, wellness culture transformation, and behavior modification. His twenty-five years of programs, services, published writings, and inspirational talks have motivated thousands of individuals from the Pacific to the Atlantic. Dan has consulted and presented at Fortune 500 companies, non-profit organizations, public and private schools, cities and counties, universities, community centers, churches, hospitals and cruise ships. Dan served as the Lead Pastor at Palo Alto First Christian Church for over five years and serves on the faculty at San Jose State University, teaching courses in Fitness and Nutrition, Health in Later Life, Team Building, Children's Health and Fitness, Stress Management, Creating a Meaningful Life, and Development of Human Potential. Dan holds a master's degree in Kinesiology with an emphasis in Gerontology from SJSU.

Lastly, Dan is blessed to be a husband to Annette and a father to Sierra and Cayden.

# Acknowledgments

This book was an amazing community effort. On August 11, 2020, I launched a thirty-day Kickstarter campaign and by September 11, 2020, I had raised over $32,000 with over 160 supporters. It is my pleasure to send all of you copies of this book as you purchased a variety of different packages in support of this project. Below are personal acknowledgments to those of you that gave at a level of $500 or more. So many others gave anywhere between $1 and $400. Please know that I am so grateful and humbled by every single contribution. You all are an absolute blessing and I pray there is a 100x return on your treasure. God bless every one of you.

**Gifts of $500+**

Brian and Linda Bishop
Matt Chad and Family
Harry and Jane Casler
Molly Carpenter
Trinh and Khanh Nguyen
Beth Fraker
John Toner
Becky Snell and Kids

## Gifts of $1,000+

Maxine Chan and Family
Annette, Sierra, and Cayden McClure
Stacy & Lexi McAllister
Pete Snell
Ryan and Erin Oto
Bill and Jen Beaton
Wade and Liz Fluckey
Jim Colvin and Family
Aaron and Kim Fluckey
Jesse and Rachel Tharp
Mom and Dad Fluckey
Mom and Dad McClure

## Gifts of $3,000+

Dave and Jen McClure
Frank and Rebecca Benaderet
Not So Small Small Group